MOTORCYCLES
WE LOVED IN THE
1970^S

PHIL WEST

The History Press

Front cover images clockwise from left: 1973 Yamaha FS1-E
(Yamaha); 1976 BMW R100RS (BMW); 1972 Kawasaki Z1 900
(Kawasaki)

Back cover images top to bottom: BMW's R90S was one of the
best European attempts to fend off the invasion of Japanese
superbikes (BMW); Paul Smart's victory in the 1972 Imola 200
ushered in a whole new era of Ducati V-twin sportsters (Ducati)

First published 2022
Reprinted 2024

The History Press
97 St George's Place, Cheltenham,
Gloucestershire, GL50 3QB
www.thehistorypress.co.uk

© Phil West, 2022

The right of Phil West to be identified as the Author
of this work has been asserted in accordance with the
Copyright, Designs and Patents Act 1988.

British Library Cataloguing in Publication Data.
A catalogue record for this book is available from the British Library.

ISBN 978 0 7509 9612 9

Typesetting and origination by The History Press
Printed in India by Thomson Press Ltd

Opposite: Motorcycle performance entered a different
dimension in the 1970s via a new breed of multi-cylindered
two- and four-stroke Japanese superbikes such as
Kawasaki's infamous 750 triple, pictured here. (Kawasaki)

Overleaf: Technology advanced rapidly, too. In 1976, BMW
introduced the first fully faired, mass-market machine – the
R100RS. It was tested in a wind tunnel with the assistance of
Pininfarina in Italy. (BMW)

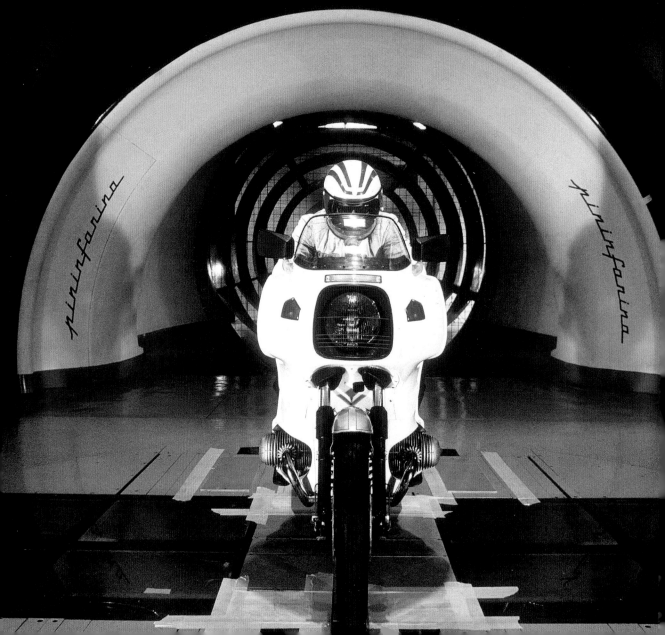

CONTENTS

ABOUT THE AUTHOR

Phil West is one of the UK's best-known and longest-established motorcycle journalists and authors. His thirty-plus-year career at the top of the profession has included being editor of leading magazines *Bike* and *What Bike?* as well as *American Motorcycles* and *Biking Times*. He was also executive editor at *Motor Cycle News*. As a freelancer, his work has been published around the globe in publications varying from *Stuff* to *FHM*, and he remains a regular contributor to *MCN*, *Bike*, *Visordown*, *Autotrader* and others. During this time, he has ridden and written about virtually every new bike.

He is also a prolific and successful author of motorcycling books, ranging from acclaimed histories of the Yamaha RD350LC, Honda Gold Wing and BMW GS, to the sister title to this book, *Motorcycles We Loved in the 1980s*.

ACKNOWLEDGEMENTS

The author would like to thank a few individuals for their help and support in producing this book. My wife, Sarah, again for her support, tolerance and occasional biscuit while I toil away at the keyboard; my late dad for encouraging and facilitating my first forays into publishing; my late mum whose grasp of English was always better than mine; and, finally, Amy Rigg and all at The History Press for having the confidence to help me make this book happen.

INTRODUCTION

When it comes to great decades in motorcycling, few are as momentous, and memorable, as the 1970s.

In terms of significance, superstars and stunning bikes, it had it all. The shift from the swinging '60s into the glam-rock '70s mirrored a similar shift in motorcycling. The traditional and historic British bike manufacturers such as Triumph, BSA and Norton were in terminal decline, replaced by rampant Japanese brands Honda, Kawasaki, Yamaha and Suzuki. As such there was a 'last hurrah' of great British bikes, including the Triumph Trident 750 and Norton JPS Replica, before they were overtaken, quite literally, by a new breed of four-cylinder 'superbikes' from the Far East, such as the CB750, Z1, XS750 and GS1000. At the same time the great European marques came up with some of their greatest bikes, including the Ducati 750 Super Sport, Moto Guzzi Le Mans, BMW R100RS and Laverda Jota. All of these bikes are featured here.

Bikes were big in popular culture, too. Movies such as 1971's *On Any Sunday*, heroes such as Evel Knievel and TV shows such as *CHiPs* brought bikes into the mainstream like never before.

1970s learners may have been restricted to 250cc, but they'd never had it so good with a range of ever-faster Japanese two-strokes, including Kawasaki's three-cylinder S1 (later renamed KH250). (Kawasaki)

Nor was the 1970s just about 'big' bikes. The UK's 1971 'sixteener' law directly spawned a new breed of hugely popular entry-level machine – the 50cc sports moped, exemplified by the Yamaha FS1-E 'Fizzy', while Japanese learner 'stroker' 250s such as Yamaha's RD250 twin and Kawasaki's KH250 triple proved equally popular for those aged 17 and over with L-plates.

The 1970s was also a golden era for bike sport, particularly in Britain (although now on largely Japanese machines). 'Scrambles' on TV evolved into motocross with the UK's Graham Noyce becoming world champion before the decade's end. Trials and speedway brought other British world-beaters, and road racing provided the

The late 1970s saw a bike-sport sensation when in 1978, Mike Hailwood, GP star of the 1960s, made a fairy-tale return to the Isle of Man TT and won on the Sports Motorcycles-entered NCR Ducati. (Ducati)

stage for Barry Sheene, the biggest of them all. The Isle of Man also saw its greatest ever story, with the comeback victory ride of Mike 'The Bike' Hailwood at the 1978 TT.

But it's the bikes themselves that are best remembered, and which illustrate a decade of development that changed motorcycling forever.

The fifty motorcycles in this book were all hugely loved throughout the 1970s, either because of their technology, style or performance. Some were and remain household names, while others were short-lived exotica reserved for an exclusive few. This book hopes to convey exactly why they were loved and lusted over during this special decade.

EUROPE'S LAST HURRAHS

BMW was just one of the historic European manufacturers who were struggling in the early 1970s against the new wave of Japanese machines. Its sporty 1973 R90S, however, did buy it some time. (BMW)

TRIUMPH TRIDENT 750, 1968

The Triumph Trident 750 was supposed to be, along with sister BSA Rocket3, the new three-cylinder superbike that would be a 1970s world leader. Unfortunately it was quickly overtaken by Honda's more powerful and modern, four-cylinder CB750. (Triumph)

Oh, what might have been.

Although not strictly a machine born in the 1970s, the Trident lived on until 1976 and symbolises early '70s biking by being both representative of the last days of the once-dominant British industry and as the unfulfilled foil to the rise of the Japanese, the 750cc triple being comprehensively trumped by Honda's CB750 four.

It could have been so different. If Triumph had progressed quicker, the Trident might have been on the market by the mid-'60s, beating Honda to the punch. Instead, although the 58bhp Trident was available shortly before the Honda, it was known the CB750 was on its way and, at 68bhp, it was more powerful, $300 cheaper, better equipped and, for many, better looking, too. So, while at best only 5,000 Tridents were produced a year, Honda were making ten times the number of CBs. No wonder Triumph never really recovered.

The Powerchoice

The New
750 Trident T160

A later, better-received restyle with the addition of disc brakes, electric start and left-foot gear change improved things, but by then it was a case of too little, too late. (Triumph)

WHAT THEY SAID

'An awesome number of people will find that third cylinder irresistible. Single and twin cylinder bikes are commonplace; even Fours are offered by more than one manufacturer. But there is only one Three.'

Cycle World, October 1968, on the $1,745 Triumph Trident T150

A Triumph triple had originally been considered as early as 1963, but the first prototype wasn't completed until 1965, the first of many delays that blighted the whole project. Triumph owners BSA then wanted their own version, the Rocket3, and demanded an engine distinguished by cylinders canted forward 10 degrees, causing further delays. Designers Ogle – later celebrated for the Raleigh Chopper and Bond Bug – were commissioned for its styling, resulting in widely disliked 'shoebox' panels, 'ray gun' silencers, an extra 18kg in weight and even more delays. Add on labour disputes and a complex assembly process, and it was a wonder the Trident ever surfaced at all.

Yet the Trident wasn't a bad bike, particularly after later restyles and updates. In 1971, both got a restyle, fifth gear and disc brake (although with BSA closing that year few Rocket3s were built). Then, in November 1974, the T150V was succeeded by the further restyled T160, with BSA-style forward-sloping cylinders, left-foot gearchange, rear disc and electric start. Finally, the Trident was the bike it always should have been.

Although not a winner on the street, the Trident did achieve success on track, most notably winning five successive Production TTs in the form of a special racer called 'Slippery Sam'. (Triumph)

It also had significant success on track, most famously as 'Slippery Sam' winning five consecutive production TTs between 1971 and 1975. At the 1971 Daytona 200 (after infamously being beaten by Honda's CB750 the previous year), a Triumph/BSA team on Rob North-framed specials swept the podium, while the same team shortly after inspired the creation of the Transatlantic Trophy. All of that, plus the fact it was the last major motorcycle from Meriden Triumph, is enough for the Trident to have achieved classic status today.

WHO LOVED IT?

The Trident/Rocket3 wasn't a failure. It was lusted after on road (even 1969 'James Bond' George Lazenby rode one) and succeeded on track. But as a commercial proposition it was leapfrogged and undercut by Honda's CB750. By 1976 just 27,480 had been made. Over 500,000 Honda CB750s were made in (roughly) the same period.

HONDA CB750, 1969

Although unveiled in 1968 and on sale in 1969, Honda's revolutionary CB750 four was the bike that paved the way for the rise of the Japanese marques that went on to dominate 1970s motorcycling. (Honda)

Just over a year shy of the start of the 1970s, an all-new machine was launched that changed motorcycling forever.

Unveiled on 28 October 1968 at the Tokyo Show, Honda's revolutionary CB750 was not only the first mass-produced motorcycle with four cylinders, but also the first with a disc brake and electric starter. It was the fastest, most powerful and sophisticated bike of its day and it quickly became known as the world's first superbike, ushering in an era of Japanese dominance that sounded the death knell for the ailing British industry.

By 1966, Honda was already the world's largest motorcycle manufacturer, but its biggest bike was 450cc and sales were falling in the US where people preferred 750cc+ Harleys or British twins.

So, in early 1967, prompted by the decision of GP's governing body to ban the multi-cylinder four-strokes Honda had been so successful with, Honda pulled out and decided to instead use its technology on larger road bikes that would appeal in the US.

WHAT THEY SAID

'Some will say it is too heavy or that four cylinders is too many for a motorcycle. But the total is greater than the sum of its parts. If the Four didn't run faster than 120mph, if it didn't turn a 100-mph standing quarter-mile, it would still be the finest.'

Cycle World, August 1969, on the $1,495 Honda CB750

The CB boasted not just the world's first mass-produced four-cylinder engine but also 68bhp, the first mainstream disc brake and electric starter. No wonder it was quickly called the first 'superbike'. (Honda)

The idea for a 750 came from Soichiro Honda himself who, in Switzerland, saw a policeman riding what he thought was a small motorcycle only to realise it was a Triumph 750. Soon afterwards, he visited American Honda and mentioned to service manager Bob Hansen they were working on a top secret 'King of Motorcycles'. Hansen knew Triumph were developing a 750 triple and responded that the new bike 'better not be a twin', suggesting instead it be a four. So, by October 1967, the basics of being a 750 producing at least 67bhp (1bhp more than Harley's then 1300) in a transverse-four arrangement with four-into-four exhaust reminiscent of Honda's multi-cylinder GP machines, was settled.

A prototype proved so fast it led directly to the adoption of the new disc brakes, then becoming popular in racing. Then, when presented to US dealers with a projected price of just $1,295 – $1,000 less than any rival – it sparked so many orders that the price was promptly raised to $1,495.

Even so, orders far surpassed the 1,500 machines first projected annually (in fact it quickly rose to 3,000 a *month*) and the CB proved a success not just on the road but in racing too, where it won the Daytona 200 the following March.

All of that helped establish the transverse-four as the new superbike template, spawning a whole family of Honda spin-offs (including the CB550, CB500 and CB400), while 750 itself survived up to 1978.

WHO LOVED IT?

Fast, sophisticated and affordable, the CB750 was a huge hit, particularly in the US, and far exceeded even Honda's own sales projections. It also remained in production for almost a decade, by which time nearly 500,000 had been built.

Early CB750s, which featured sand-cast engine cases, are today among the most collectable (and valuable) of all Japanese motorcycles. (Honda)

YAMAHA XS650, 1969

Worthy rather than revolutionary, the Yamaha XS650 still deserves exalted status for two reasons: firstly, by being a Japanese interpretation of an inherently British engine design (an air-cooled, 650cc parallel-twin), the XS's performance, reliability and durability was the most solid indication yet of what the emerging Japanese manufacturers could get right (and the failing British were getting wrong). Secondly, by being two-stroke specialist Yamaha's biggest (by far) four-stroke to date, the XS650 laid the foundations for all future Yamaha four-strokes to follow.

Unveiled at the Tokyo Show in October 1969 before going on sale in early 1970, the XS-1 (as originally called) was aimed directly at traditional British twins such as the T120 Bonneville. Underneath that familiar layout, however, was the most advanced engine in the class.

WHAT THEY SAID

'The XS650 must be considered a success having supplied all the ingredients required to please the big twin fancier in an up-to-date and beautifully styled package. It looks good, rides good, stays clean and shows few of the faults one would expect in a first-year model.'

Cycle World, March 1970, on the $1,245 Yamaha XS650

Opposite: Honda rival Yamaha's first Europe-challenging big four-stroke was the XS-1 (later XS650) as unveiled in late 1969 before going on sale in 1970. (Yamaha)

More conventional than Honda's revolutionary CB750, the XS650 was a 'British-style' 650cc parallel-twin but with a number of key upgrades, including horizontally split crankcases that improved reliability. (Yamaha)

Developed using expertise gained working with Toyota on its GT2000 sports car (as in the 1967 James Bond film *You Only Live Twice*), it featured a chain-driven single overhead cam (most British rivals still used pushrod-operated overhead valves), novel roller-bearing bottom end and horizontally (rather than vertically, as used by the Brits) split crankcases.

The result produced 53bhp (compared to the then Bonneville T120's 49), and although the Yamaha didn't handle or look as good as the Triumph, it was more reliable, durable and, crucially, cheaper.

A steady seller, particularly in the US, it achieved race success in the hands of Kenny Roberts in US flat track and was steadily developed, adding an electric start in 1972. It was renamed the XS650 in 1975 and remained in production, latterly in cruiser 'Special' style, until 1985.

Later versions gained a disc front brake and electric starter while variants included a custom version which proved popular in the US. The XS650 was a big success throughout the 1970s before finally being deleted in 1983. (Yamaha)

WHO LOVED IT?

Affordable, a good performer and reliable, the XS made massive inroads into a US market traditionally reserved for big British parallel twins, hastening the likes of Triumph and BSA's demise. An estimated 500,000 were produced up to 1983.

MV AGUSTA 750 SPORT, 1970

Italian legends MV Agusta may have dominated 500cc Grand Prix in the 1960s but they were slow to capitalise with a road version. It finally came in 1970 with the phenomenal 750 S. (MV Agusta)

In 1970 Italian legends MV Agusta were at the top of their luxurious, exotic, high-performance game, even if most mere mortals couldn't get close to affording one.

As 500cc Grand Prix world champions for the thirteenth year in succession, their stock in trade was high-performance, DOHC, transverse four-cylinder 500cc engines. But the Varese firm

A later version, the 1975 America, with more modern styling, twin disc brakes and increased power, was even more desirable and today is among the most valuable of 1970s classics. (MV Agusta)

WHAT THEY SAID

'This motorcycle is an ego pump guaranteed to convert the most circumspect motorcyclist into a flaming exhibitionist. The MV Agusta Sport never lets you forget that, after all the measurements have been taken, all the data collected, all the figures tabulated, motorcycles are an emotional experience.'

Cycle magazine, September 1973, on the £2,000 MV Agusta 750 S

didn't offer a production version for the street until 1965 and, wary of bikes being converted into racers, made that version a 600cc tourer with shaft drive.

That bike's failure prompted its replacement in 1970 with a pure sports machine bored out to 743cc, producing 72bhp (four more than Honda's CB750) and capable of 120mph, making it one of the fastest, if not the fastest, bikes of the day. It looked the part, too, with a big, twin-leading-shoe front drum brake, Ceriani forks and race-style seat and tank.

An even more desirable fully faired version, the 750 SS, was introduced in 1971. But the ultimate incarnation was surely the 1975–77 750 S America, built at the behest of MV's US importer, with a further 2mm overbore taking it to 789cc and 75bhp, uprated cycle parts, including twin front discs, and new, more angular bodywork closer to that of MV's GP racer. It had an eye-watering price tag of $6,500 to match (Honda's CB750 cost $2,190).

WHO LOVED IT?

Fast, exotic and a world championship winner, the MV 750 S had it all – including a price that put it out of reach of virtually everyone. Between 1970 and 1975, just 583 examples were made, which today are among the most valuable classics of all.

Based on an earlier 600cc four-cylinder tourer, the 1970 S was enlarged, tuned and had the very best components and brazen styling. Without the the tourer's heavy shaft drive, it was arguably the ultimate sports bike of the day. (MV Agusta)

HARLEY-DAVIDSON XR750, 1970

The XR750 was Harley's response to changes in AMA racing regulations. This first 'ironhead' version proved vulnerable to overheating but better was to come. (H-D)

Though no road bike, the significance of Harley-Davidson's XR750, launched in 1970, cannot be overstated. Winning its first AMA Flat Track title in 1972, it went on to dominate the sport for the next three decades and today, it is considered the world's most successful racing motorcycle.

It was created as a consequence of a rule change in 1969, which forced Harley to come up with a new 750cc OHV-engined racer that could compete successfully against British rivals such as BSA and Triumph.

WHO LOVED IT?

Any US flat-track racer who wanted to win, but particularly works riders Jay Springsteen (three times champion), Scott Parker (nine times champion) and Chris Carr (seven times champion). Even 1970s stunt rider Evel Knievel favoured the XR for his biggest 1970s jumps. Although just 520 bikes were built, engines were also made available to racers.

The improved 1971 version overcame the early overheating problems with the use of new alloy cylinder heads among other refinements. (H-D)

Among the XR750's most successful proponents was works Harley rider Jay Springsteen, who won three consecutive AMA Grand National Championships in 1976, 1977 and 1978. (H-D)

Based on the existing, Sportster-derived, 900cc unit, Harley's engineers reduced that bike's stroke and increased its bore to come in just under the 750cc limit. Unfortunately, however, those first 1970 XRs also retained iron cylinder heads, which, combined with a high 8.5:1 compression ratio and increased rpm, resulted in overheating. According to the AMA's rules, 200 were made available to the public that year at a price of $3,200.

For 1972, new aluminium heads, along with larger valves and other changes, were adopted, with the result being an impressive 82bhp at 7,700rpm, a top speed of around 115mph and no more overheating.

From its introduction that year right up to 2008, the alloy-head XR750 won twenty-nine of the thirty-seven AMA Grand National Championships and racked up more race wins than any other bike in AMA history. A road-race version, the XRTT, briefly found success in the hands of Cal Rayborn, while a street version, the XR1000, was launched in 1983 – although, costing almost double that of a standard Sportster XL, it wasn't a commercial success and was withdrawn after two years.

MOTO GUZZI V7 SPORT, 1971

The 1971 V7 Sport, a fully revamped, sportier version of the 1967 V7, established Moto Guzzi as a credible superbike brand, paving the way for the 1976 Le Mans 850 and more. (Moto Guzzi)

It's often forgotten that the engine Moto Guzzi is most known for – the transverse-mounted, shaft-drive V-twin – wasn't actually introduced until the late 1960s. The first, the 700cc V7, arrived in 1967 and was reasonably well received. That was succeeded by the enlarged 748cc V7 Ambassador in 1969, conceived to be a rival for Harley-Davidson in the US. But it wasn't until the configuration was given a makeover and an all-new chassis to create the V7 Sport in 1971 that Guzzi V-twins were considered credible sports machines, paving the way for a generation of Guzzis, including the legendary Le Mans, that define the brand today.

Although still fairly heavy, the V7 Sport produced a credible 70bhp, enough for a top speed of almost 130mph. (Moto Guzzi)

WHAT THEY SAID

'Although the V7 Sport has sporting features it can be used for touring and long trips without tiring the rider ... it really is a motorcycle which means something in today's motorcycling world, and even if the price is a little high it will surely be accepted by two-wheeled enthusiasts everywhere.'

Two Wheels magazine (Australia), December 1972, on the $AUS 2,696 Moto Guzzi V7 Sport

The V7 Sport was the brainchild of Lino Tonti, who took over as Guzzi's head of design at the historic factory at Mandello del Lario on the banks of Lake Como in 1970. Tonti saw the potential for a performance machine based around the touring V-twin engine so created a stiffer and lighter frame, reworked the motor's heads to boost power by 7bhp and created all-new, sleek bodywork dominated by a 17-litre fuel tank, now considered one of the most beautiful ever created.

It worked too. Although expensive and quite heavy, the V7 Sport was fast, fine handling and proved such a strong seller that it led directly to the 1976 Le Mans, Monza and more. Its uprated 748cc engine, meanwhile, formed the basis of most big-bore Guzzis to come. In 2008, when Guzzi was looking for inspiration for its own rival to Triumph's revived Bonneville retro roadster, it chose the V7 and quickly followed it with a lime-green V7 Café Classic. Today, the 1971 V7 Sport is considered one of the most collectable and significant Guzzis of all.

The engine's heads were reworked, the chassis was lighter and stiffer and all-new bodywork helped to set a style Guzzi would adhere to for decades to come. (Moto Guzzi)

WHO LOVED IT?

The first true sports bike from Moto Guzzi's big V-twin era, the V7 Sport ushered in a new era for the Italian marque highlighted by the more famous Le Mans. The V7 Sport, though significant, remained a niche machine, with just 3,142 bikes built.

DUCATI 750 GT, 1971

Moto Guzzi wasn't the only Italian brand exploring the popularity of the new 750 class. The 750 GT was Ducati's first 90-degree V-twin, created by mating two Ducati singles on a common crankcase. (Ducati)

Although Paul Smart's 1972 Imola-winning Ducati 750 V-twin is rightly celebrated for setting the Italian marque on a new course of 'desmo' V-twin sporting success, while its road-going replica, the 750 Super Sport, is today the most collectable Bologna-built bike of all, Ducati's road-going V-twin heritage actually begins elsewhere – with the 1971 750 GT.

The longitudinal V-twin layout helped keep the GT slim. And although fairly long, quality cycle parts helped ensure the new Ducati V-twin was a good handler. (Ducati)

WHAT THEY SAID

'When the disc brake squeezes the bike down from three-figure speeds, when the right peg nicks down in an 80mph sweeper and the bike never bobbles, when the 750 leaps forward from 3,000 rpm in fourth cog, then you know. You know a motorcyclist designed this machine and he got it right.'

Cycle magazine, October 1972, on the $1995 Ducati 750 GT

It's often forgotten that up to the mid-1960s Ducati largely built lightweights and was most famous for its sporty and scrambler-style singles, as designed by Fabio Taglioni.

In 1964, however, at the request of its US importers, Ducati created a 1,200cc V-twin prototype, the Apollo, intended to rival Harley-Davidson. That project proved defunct, but when Honda unveiled its CB750 in 1968, Ducati realised larger, multi-cylinder machines were the future and tasked Taglioni to create a new engine to lead into a new era.

What Taglioni came up with was brilliant but simple. He mated two bevel-drive 350 singles together at 90 degrees on a common crankshaft,

The Italian firm's new flagship helped propel Ducati into being one of the most fashionable and desirable European brands of the early 1970s. (Ducati)

creating the first 'Ducati trademark' 'L-twin'. His design was finished by March 1970, a first prototype was tested in July and, just sixty days later in September, the first bikes were made available to the Italian press, who were promptly blown away.

Although it required a fairly long chassis, the 90-degree layout gave perfect primary balance, ensuring the new GT was smooth. It was also slim, surprisingly light at just 185kg and, with quality Marzocchi forks and Lockheed disc brakes, had excellent handling and braking.

On sale the following spring, the 750 GT was a hit from the outset and its success encouraged Ducati to follow it up with the 750 Sport the following year, which, along with Smart's success in that year's Imola 200 aboard the racing, desmodromic version, inspired the 1973 750 Super Sport. It was the start of a whole new Ducati era and association with a particular type of engine it retains to this day.

Although it used a 'bevel drive' valve actuation system rather than the desmodromics Ducati would soon become most associated with, the GT was key for establishing the success of the V-twin layout. (Ducati)

WHO LOVED IT?

Although no sportster, the GT was Ducati's first 750 L-twin and a significant step into the big time for the Italian marque. A total of 4,133 were built.

SUZUKI GT750, 1971

Honda may have been the first of the Japanese manufacturers to revolutionise 1970s motorcycling with a new breed of 750cc, multi-cylinder superbike, but it certainly wasn't the last.

Kawasaki would famously enter the 'four-stroke four' fray in 1972 with its Z1 900, but before then there were two more equally significant 750 'multis' – both of them two-stroke.

Suzuki's GT750, unveiled at the Tokyo Show at the end of 1970, came first. At 738cc, its all-new three-cylinder engine was the largest two-stroke yet while it also pioneered water-cooling, which led to its nickname of 'the kettle'.

However, although it was targeted at Honda's 68bhp CB, the slightly cumbersome 67bhp GT was more 'Grand Tourer' (hence its name) than sporty superbike so never quite snatched Honda's crown.

Suzuki was the next of the ambitious Japanese factories to threaten the Europeans with a powerful 750 – but this time with a two-stroke triple, the GT750. (Suzuki)

WHAT THEY SAID

'Watercooling, fantastic brakes, good electrics and comfort for £882 must make the Suzuki the best value for money going in the 750 class.'

Bike magazine, November 1974, on the £882 Suzuki GT750

The GT's water cooling was revolutionary, leading to its 'Kettle' and 'Water buffalo' nicknames. Later versions also gained twin front disc brakes. (Suzuki)

It was still a success, however. The GT was smooth, torquey and lavish, equipped with an electric starter and twin discs as early as a 1973 makeover. It lived on until 1978 as Suzuki's flagship, gaining thousands of fans with its alternative, 'stroker superbike' style.

It had more than a little success in sport, too. A racing version, the TR750, debuted in 1972, and, despite notoriously wayward handling, the 120bhp machine was one of the fastest racers of the early 1970s. In 1973 it propelled new Suzuki star Barry Sheene to the F750 title. Less gloriously, it was also the bike he was riding in his infamous Daytona 200 crash at 170mph in 1975.

Refined power

The GT750 has a high-performance 2-stroke, 3 cylinder engine that delivers 70HP at 6,500 rpm. Electric and kick starting. And a 5-speed gearbox to maximize the power efficiency. CCI lubrication oils the crankshaft, connecting rod bearings, cylinders and cylinder head, efficiently and according to your speed.

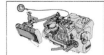

Liquid cooling

Suzuki's liquid cooling means smoothness, reliability, and a quiet ride at high speeds. And the lightweight aluminum radiator means an optimum cooling effect. In this Suzuki design, the pump gets important cooling to the cylinder block and cylinder head for outstanding open-road cooling efficiency.

Braking refinement

The GT750 is lots more than easy, agile handling. It's also maximum braking power for safe stops. Double front disc brakes give powerful braking in combination with a mechanical leading/trailing shoe brake on the rear wheel.

Instruments

In addition to speedometer, water temperature gauge, tachometer and tripmeter, the GT750 has a digital gear indicator that helps you keep cruising efficiency always at prime. And the entire cluster is rubber dampened to prevent vibration and make for easy, at-a-glance reading.

Switches

Everything is easily accessible. One the left end of the handlebar are headlamp on and off and high/low beam switch, turn signals switch, horn button, and passing light switch. On the other end is the engine kill switch and cell button.

Maui Blue Metallic

Flake Orange

Maximum Speed:	192–200 kph (120–125 mph)
Maximum Horsepower:	70.0 hp/6,500 rpm S.A.E. NET
Maximum Torque:	8.5 kg-m (61.5 ft-lb)/ 5,500 rpm
Engine Type:	2-stroke, liquid cooled, 3 cylinder
Piston Displacement:	738 cc (45.0 cu-in)
Transmission:	5-speed, constant mesh
Fuel Tank Capacity:	17.0 ltr (4.5/3.7 US/Imp gal)
Lubrication:	Suzuki CCI
Overall Length:	2,205 mm (86.5 in)
Overall Width:	880 mm (34.6 in)
Overall Height:	1,125 mm (44.3 in)
Ground Clearance:	140 mm (5.5 in)
Suspension:	
Front:	Telescopic, oil-dampened
Rear:	Oil-dampened, 5-way adjustable
Tyres, Front:	3.25H19-4PR
Rear:	4.00H18-4PR
Dry Weight:	230 kg (507 lbs)
Starter:	Electric and kick
Colours:	Maui Blue Metallic Flake Orange

*Specifications subject to change without notice.

Repeatedly updated and restyled, the GT, although no pure sportster, proved a big success in the 1970s for its performance and value before going out of production in 1977. (Suzuki)

WHO LOVED IT?

Suzuki's biggest bike of the early 1970s, although too heavy to be a sportster, was popular with techies (as the first with a liquid-cooled engine) and two-stroke fans, with around 71,000 sold worldwide up to 1977.

One of the biggest challengers to the European status quo in the early 1970s was another wild two-stroke triple – Kawasaki's phenomenal 750cc Mach IV. (Kawasaki)

Bikes don't get more outrageous or more '1970s' than Kawasaki's hooligan, ballistic, polluting, uneconomic, horribly handling and downright brilliant 750 Mach IV.

The second of that year's stroker superbikes, the Mach IV was powerful, smelly (it was infamous for bellowing blue smoke as its mpg fell to below 20) and fast – terrifyingly so.

Kawasaki had stunned the motorcycling world with its 500cc H1 Mach III in 1969, a riotous two-stroke triple producing 60bhp. For 1972, however, inspired by both Honda's CB750 and the newly formed Formula 750 production-based race series, the 750cc Mach IV was almost inevitable.

An enlarged version of the 500, it was a 748cc, piston-ported, air-cooled triple, but boy did it deliver. Peak power was 74bhp (when, by comparison, Triumph's latest Trident 750 produced just 58) while it weighed just 8kg more than the H1.

The result, in 1972, was simply sensational. Kawasaki itself boldly stated in its brochure: 'We've pulled a fast one on the competition. Of all the world's production models it's the fastest thing on two wheels. Faster than any Suzuki. Faster than any Triumph. Faster than any BSA, and any Honda, any anything.'

They weren't wrong. The trouble was, that power rush all came at once in a narrow powerband and the spindly, lightweight chassis could barely cope. It flexed in corners, weaved on

An enlarged, updated version of the previous 500cc H1 Mach III, the H2 Mach IV was Kawasaki's response to the popularity of 750s such as the Trident and CB750 and new F750 racing class. They also built a wild H2R racer. (Kawasaki)

WHAT THEY SAID

'After going into a horrifying tankslapper at 115mph the friction damper was tightened down to get the H2 safely through the lights at 120mph, which is exactly what the speedo read.'

Bike magazine, March/April 1973, on the £754 Kawasaki H2 750 Mach IV

The most powerful 750 superbike

With 74bhp, the fastest acceleration of any bike and yet an infamously wayward chassis, the Mach IV also earned another nickname – 'The Widowmaker'. (Kawasaki)

the straights and was so prone to wheelies it soon earned the nickname 'Widowmaker'.

A racing version, the H2R, also debuted in 1972, and in its striking 'Green Meanie' livery in the hands of the likes of Canadian Yvon Duhamel, Gary Nixon in the US and Mick Grant and Barry Ditchburn in the UK, it became a fixture of early 1970s racing.

For 1974 the road version was improved to become the H2 with chassis and engine mods. But with the arrival of Kawasaki's Z1 900, plus the 1973 oil crisis, which prompted increasingly strict environmental and emissions regulations, the 22mpg H2's days were numbered and the last bike was built in 1975. Today, however, the brilliant but bonkers H2, which became the 'daddy' of Kawasaki's five bike, two-stroke triple Tri-Star line up of the S1 250, S2 350, S3 400 and H1 500, is among the most collectable of its machines, with auction prices regularly above £20,000.

WHO LOVED IT?

The fastest accelerating road bike of its day, the bonkers, hooligan H2 was the dream bike of headbangers before falling foul of emissions and high fuel consumption. An estimated 47,000 of all types were built.

In the early 1970s, if you were 17 or without a full licence, but still wanted a Kawasaki two-stroke triple, the S1 250 was for you. (Kawasaki)

In the 1970s one of the most popular classes, due to the prevailing learner law, was for two-stroke sports 250s, whether they be Yamaha RDs or Suzuki GTs. At the same time, the most outrageous sports stroker of the early 1970s was Kawasaki's 750 triple, the Mach IV. Marry those two factors together and you get one of the most fondly remembered bikes of the '70s – Kawasaki's S1 250 triple, later renamed the KH250.

The S1 was launched in early 1972 as the final member of Kawasaki's Tri-Star family of two-stroke triples. It matched its bigger brothers' styling, and also came complete with a sexy tailpiece that would take rival factories years to replicate.

But in truth it wasn't that advanced. Its engine lacked the disc valves of its predecessor, it was heavy and its drum front brake struggled to haul the bike up.

But with 32bhp, it could reach almost 100mph and it had one thing no other 250 could match – *three* cylinders like the madcap 750, plus a soundtrack that was simply unique.

WHAT THEY SAID

'Although it's been slowed a bit it's still the most sophisticated package in the 250 class, the third cylinder doesn't cost you any extra in either price or fuel consumption and it handles.'

Bike magazine, June 1974, on the £510 Kawasaki S1 250

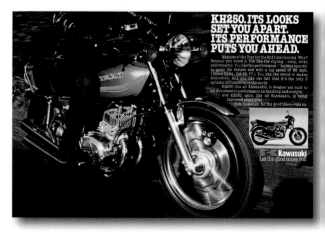

Later renamed the KH250, the S1 was one of the fastest 'learner 250s' of the early 1970s and, with styling including a pioneering, faired-in 'tail piece', was also one of the best looking. (Kawasaki)

Yes, it had overheating problems. Yes, its chassis and brakes weren't a match for Yamaha's RD twin. And yes, it could be thirsty, with mpg dropping as low as 22. But the triple gave a unique aural experience and was as close as any 17-year-old could get to the wild 750 Mach IV. For many, that was enough.

By the end of the 1970s, however, the KH250 was the only Kawasaki triple left, its final year being 1981. The 350, followed by the 400, lasted until 1979, and 1975 saw the end of the Mach IV while the Mach 1 500, renamed KH500 in 1976, lasted only until 1977. But boy, they were glorious while they did.

The KH250 remained in production throughout the decade right up to 1981. By then, however, against the likes of Yamaha's new RD250LC it was looking quite dated, despite Kawasaki's efforts. (Kawasaki)

WHO LOVED IT?

As the entry-level, learner-legal version of Kawasaki's two-stroke triple family, the S1/KH proved a big hit with teenagers dreaming of an H2. An estimated 48,000 of all types were built.

KAWASAKI Z1 900, 1972

Honda's CB750 may have been the first superbike, introducing the four-cylinder format that would dominate motorcycling over the next decade, but the Z1, which followed from rivals Kawasaki, was every bit as significant.

When Honda unveiled the CB in late 1968, Kawasaki's own 750-four was almost complete. Stunned, Honda's rival immediately scrapped its newcomer and went back to the drawing board, determined to outdo the CB. The project

Kawasaki's delayed response to Honda's CB750 was arguably the most desirable and significant of all 1970s superbikes – the mighty Z1 900. (Kawasaki)

took three years, cheekily involved the use of prototypes disguised as Hondas, and resulted in the Z1 900 in late 1972.

At 903cc, with twin cams producing a whopping 82bhp, the 'Zed' was bigger, more sophisticated and more powerful than the CB750, establishing a new superbike benchmark it would retain for five years.

That monster engine, and its resulting performance, tells you all you need to know about the Z1. Following the unveiling of the CB750, Kawasaki's new machine was conceived to be 'King of Motorcycles' and to not just beat the Honda – but decimate it. So, although also an air-cooled four, the Z1 had oversquare bore and stroke dimensions compared to the traditional long-stroke Honda, twin camshafts, more sophisticated bucket-and-shim adjusters and also a five-speed gearbox.

Kawasaki also took no chances in proving the Z1's durability and reliability. In late 1972, it rented Talledega Speedway and ran test mules flat out for entire tankfuls of fuel.

Soon after its launch, Kawasaki ramped up publicity further by taking its new baby (and factory riders Yvon Duhamel, Art Baumann and Gary Nixon) to Daytona after that year's 200 race, where, over two days, it set a new world speed record by averaging 109.6mph for twenty-four hours.

It was all enough for it to become an instant sensation and immediately establish itself as the new performance king. It was also voted 'Machine of the Year' by readers of the UK's *MCN* not just once but four years in succession. 'King of Motorcycles'? Not half.

Conceived as the 'King of Kings', the all-new, four-cylinder 'Zed' was not only bigger than the Honda, it was more sophisticated, better equipped and significantly more powerful with double overhead cams. (Kawasaki)

WHO LOVED IT?

The new superbike king, the Z1 was loved not just by '70s riders wanting the ultimate street bike but also drag racers, specials builders and more. Reputedly inspiring Suzuki's own GS750/1000, it remained in production until being updated by the 1975 Z900, by which time an estimated 85,000 had been built.

The original, 'black-engined', 1972 Z1 produced 82bhp – 14 more than the CB750, so becoming motorcycling's performance king for most of the decade. (Kawasaki)

The Z1 was updated to become the Z1A, then Z1B and then the Z900 in 1975, although it was essentially the same bike throughout. (Kawasaki)

HONDA XL250, 1972

By the early 1970s, lightweight two-strokes, both from Japan and Europe, had taken over the off-road motorcycle world. Honda changed all that with the revolutionary four-stroke XL250. (Honda)

Apart from the rise of a new breed of multi-cylinder Japanese superbike, early 1970s motorcycling was also characterised by another two-wheeled trend – the huge popularity of dual purpose 'trail' bikes.

But there was one manufacturer conspicuous by its absence. While the European manufacturers offered machines like the four-stroke Ducati Scrambler, and Yamaha and Suzuki had two-stroke 250s such as the DT2 and TS250, the biggest of the Japanese 'Big Four', Honda, had nothing. That all changed with the XL250.

WHAT THEY SAID

'The XL250 is destined to become one of the most popular off-road motorcycles ever.'

Cycle World, 1972, on the $850 Honda XL250

The XL was an all-new design which steadfastly stayed true to Honda's heritage in being a four-stroke amidst a sea of screaming strokers. To compete, the XL had the first mass-produced overhead camshaft, four-valve engine while its cylinder and cases were aluminium (with side covers in even more exotic magnesium) to keep it light.

This was bolted into a single loop frame with the latest Ceriani forks, five-way adjustable twin rear shocks and aluminium-rimmed 21/18in wheels. The XL was then finished off with swoopy silver styling and paired speedo/tacho.

Despite the clever design and exotic materials, the XL was still heavier than the two-strokes, but its grunty and progressive drive more than made up for it, being particularly suited to climbing hills and traversing trails. In fact the new Honda was such a good 'trailie' that it instantly became the new benchmark and a huge commercial success throughout the 1970s. It spawned a host of larger versions and imitators, such as Honda's XL500 and Yamaha's XT250 and 500, which became the dominant trail bikes of the early 1980s.

The XL was highlighted by a pioneering, purpose-built, lightweight OHC single-cylinder engine fitted into a simple but clever minimalist chassis. (Honda)

WHO LOVED IT?

The first mass-produced four-stroke, four-valve single cylinder 'trail' bike, the first-generation XL was a big hit, particularly in the US, and inspired a whole new generation of on/off-road machines.

The result was easy to ride, flexible, rugged and such a big hit, particularly in the US, that it paved the way for a new generation of 1970s Japanese four-stroke trail bikes. (Honda)

BENELLI SEI 750, 1972

One European bike brand determined to make a big splash in the early 1970s was historic Italian marque Benelli with its astonishing, six-cylinder 750 Sei. (Benelli)

No motorcycle of the early 1970s was more exotic than the brilliant – but ultimately flawed – Benelli Sei. The world's first production six-cylinder came a full six years before Honda's CBX1000, yet with Italian styling and componentry and an ultra-exclusive price, the Sei married the ambitious, multi-cylinder technology of the Far East with the exotic style and specification of European machines.

As such, the Sei could – and perhaps *should* – have been the most powerful, fastest, best-handling and most desirable motorcycle of the 1970s. Instead, production delays, underwhelming performance, reliability and build-quality issues consigned it to be one of the great 'what ifs' of the decade.

It was the pet project of ambitious Argentine entrepreneur Alejandro De Tomaso. After founding the De Tomaso sports car company in Italy, which later produced the Ford V8-engined Pantera, he also took over Maserati and design houses Ghia and Vignale.

Then, in 1971, De Tomaso took over ailing Italian bike legend Benelli and promptly directed its engineers to come up with a new flagship with a six-cylinder engine, the most beautiful styling and the best of components. Upon unveiling the first prototype a little over a year later, De Tomaso famously proclaimed that he was 'declaring war on the Japanese motorcycle'.

Unfortunately, the Sei never quite delivered. Its design proved controversial in effectively being a Honda CB500/4 with two extra cylinders. Although beautiful and desirable (it was styled by Ghia), delays meant it was unattainable. And although a fine handler with quality Brembo brakes, Marzocchi forks and alloy Borrani wheels, with only 71bhp (when Kawasaki's far cheaper Z1 had 82), the Sei wasn't even fast.

WHAT THEY SAID

'It's not the fastest from stoplight to stoplight, not the quickest over Mulholland Highway, not an economy winner or a touring trickster. What it does do though, it does with the best, with a novelty appeal and sound unsurpassed by any other machine. Does that make it worth over three grand? That's kinda up to you ...'

Cycle World, January 1974, on the $3,500 Benelli Sei 750

Benelli tried again with the enlarged and restyled Sei 900 in 1978, but by then Honda's own twin-cam, 105bhp six, the CBX1000, was available. Today, however, the Sei remains one of the most remarkable and collectable 1970s Italian classics of all.

Unfortunately, however, it never quite lived up to expectations and even a later, restyled, 900cc version failed to make the Sei six cylinder a success. (Benelli)

WHO LOVED IT?

Although fabulous, price and production delays meant the Sei was a failure. Just 293 were built in 1974 with only a further 3,000 or so up to 1977. The 1978 900 wasn't a success, either, with under 2,000 built.

Under new De Tomaso ownership, the Sei was conceived to be Benelli's new flagship bike and a machine worthy of being mentioned in the same breath as automobile legends Ferrari, Maserati and Lamborghini. (Benelli)

DUCATI 750 SUPER SPORT, 1973

One of the greatest bikes of the 1970s, the 750 Super Sport was conceived as a road-going replica of the bike that famously took Brit Paul Smart to victory in the 1972 Imola 200. (Ducati)

If the Benelli Sei was the ultimate 1970s Italian motorcycling exotica, the 1973 Ducati 750 Super Sport trumped it for being the decade's most significant Italian motorcycle overall.

A limited edition, road-going replica of the 750 V-twin racer ridden to victory by Brit Paul Smart at the 1972 Imola 200, the Super Sport, as the Italian firm's first production desmo V-twin, effectively set the template for Ducati's next forty years.

In short, without the 750 Super Sport, which was unveiled in late 1973, the 851, 916, 1098 and more would never have existed.

The real significance of the Super Sport, of course, was not that it was a 'first', but that it worked so well. Based on the already impressive 748cc, 90-degree V-twin from the 750 GT, but with the desmodromic valves of the racer, it also had a raised compression ratio of 10.5:1 (up from 8.5:1) and bigger 40mm carbs, which together helped boost power to 72bhp up from the GT's 50.

Smart's victory had been completely unforeseen. The Bologna factory was then inexperienced in bigger bikes and it was competing against the likes of Giacomo Agostini on the all-dominant MV Agusta. (Ducati)

WHAT THEY SAID

'It's the definitive factory-built café racer ...
a bike that stands at the farthest reaches of
the sporting world ...'

Cycle magazine, June 1974, on the $2,105
Ducati 750 Super Sport

The road-going replica was also Ducati's first desmodromic
V-twin roadster, setting the design template the Italian marque
would adhere to rigidly for the next forty years. (Ducati)

Those features, combined with a claimed dry weight of 151kg (Kawasaki's then superbike king Z1 may have produced 84bhp but it also weighed a hefty 230kg dry), plus a fine-handling chassis with the best suspension and brakes from Marzocchi and Brembo, added up to the best-performing 750 of the day. And with a sporty riding position, racy fairing and Imola replica green/silver paint job, Ducati's new 750 was also one of the best-looking motorcycles around.

Unfortunately for Ducati, however, the 750 Super Sport, although a success, was not the money-maker it could have been. Designer Taglioni's glorious 'round case' desmo V-twin proved difficult and expensive to make, causing production delays and resulting in only 401 examples being built in 1974.

To improve things, Taglioni was asked to design a simpler bevel-drive system and Giorgetto Giugiaro of Ital Design came up with a new, 'square case' engine-case design that, together with an enlarged 864cc capacity, resulted in the 900 Super Sport of 1975.

Today, however, those short-lived, 'round-case' 750s have become some of the most collectible motorcycles of all.

Ducati didn't just win at Imola, it grabbed first and second with Brit Smart (right) beating team leader Bruno Spaggiari (left) across the line. (Ducati)

WHO LOVED IT?

Italian exotica lovers, racers, playboys, journalists ... all loved the 'SS'. Unfortunately, just 401 were built and, with many raced and crashed, far fewer survive, helping make the 750 desmo today the rarest, most desirable classic Ducati of all.

TRIUMPH BONNEVILLE T140, 1973

Although Triumph's original 1959 Bonneville T120 had proved a revelation and was a 1960s best-seller, by the early 1970s it needed a major update. The 1973 T140 was the overdue result. (Triumph)

While the original Bonneville was born in 1959 and the definitive example is often cited as the 1967 650, the 1970s saw the ultimate, fastest and, in many ways, best incarnation of the breed – the 1973 T140V. Unfortunately, it was all too little, too late.

With the rise of the Japanese marques and bikes like the CB750 and Z1, Triumph was in big trouble. Its 750 Trident had not been the success hoped for, BSA had closed completely and the outdated 650 Bonneville T120 was living on past glories. But Norton Villiers Triumph gave it, too late, one final roll of the dice in 1973 when it grew to 744cc and gained a five-speed gearbox.

Testers, slightly bamboozled by the latest Japanese leviathans and nostalgic for how bikes used to be, raved about the T140's handling. With 50bhp, it was also the briskest Bonnie yet (if not quite capable of the 140mph its name suggested).

Enlarged to 744cc, the new Bonnie was the most powerful yet with 50bhp, even if it wasn't capable of the 140mph its name suggested. It remained in production, sometimes sporadically, until 1983. (Triumph)

WHO LOVED IT?

Not many, to be honest. Although the final incarnation of the classic British twin was well received by traditionalists, most of the 1970s motorcycling world had moved onto the new generation of Japanese superbikes. Sporadic production means exact production numbers are difficult to gauge.

Sadly, however, it was also launched just as the closure of Meriden was announced, leading to an eighteen-month strike stopping all production, which only resumed under the infamous 1975 workers' co-operative. The T140 was improved further in 1976, gaining a rear disc and US-friendly left-hand gearshift, while various spin-offs, including the Silver Jubilee, were produced.

History tells us, of course, it was to no avail. The antiquated Bonnie was no match for the latest Japanese machines and Meriden Triumph was in its death throes, finally collapsing in 1983.

But the last 750 Bonnies were arguably the best of the breed, can still be had for a comparative song and ultimately helped inspire the 2000 Hinckley version that carries on motorcycling's greatest name today.

US versions featured different styling, including a 'peanut' tank, although this was also made available in the UK in 1979 with the stylish, alloy-wheeled, black and gold T140D. (Triumph)

WHAT THEY SAID

'The Bonneville 750 is not an everyman motorcycle. Its owner is a person with an explicit point of view about motorcycling and it's a motorcycle that exemplifies that. Those who don't share that viewpoint – those who have never thought of a multi-cylindered, water-cooled, vibration-free, dead reliable, solid state motorcycle as a lifeless refrigerator – will never understand.'

Cycle Guide, May 1973, on the $1,995 Triumph Bonneville T140V

BMW R90S, 1973

BMW broke out of its traditional, conservative ways in the early 1970s with its R90S – its most powerful and fastest boxer yet. With a radical handlebar fairing and brazen colour schemes, it was also its most striking. (BMW)

BMW has been inextricably linked to the shaft-drive boxer twin ever since its first bike, the R32 of 1923. During that time there have been a huge variety of models, but the best, in most experts' eyes, came in the 1970s with the 1973 R90S.

BMW Motorrad entered the 1970s facing an uncertain future. While its 1960 R69S had been a success, subsequent models seemed increasingly dated and expensive, especially compared to the new Japanese machines.

A significant step forward came with the opening of its new Berlin plant in 1969 and the launch of the significantly updated /5 series in 50, 60 and 75 forms. But BMWs were still considered dowdy touring machines and the company desperately needed a new flagship with the 'wow' factor.

To create it, BMW enlarged 1972's R75/6 to 898cc and 60bhp to be the biggest, most powerful boxer yet, the 1973 R90/6. At the same time, as with the R69S, BMW created a special 'S' version.

With 67bhp and new twin front disc brakes, the R90S had the all-round performance to give the new Japanese superbikes a run for their money and even proved successful on track. (BMW)

WHO LOVED IT?

Not only the ultimate BMW of the early '70s, the R90S was also the ultimate grand tourer with the price – and exclusivity – to match. A total of 17,465 were made.

The R90S had a higher compression ratio and bigger carbs to boost power to 67bhp. It got a second front disc and steering damper. Stylist Hans Muth was also brought in to give it a distinct identity by way of larger tank, handlebar fairing (a world first on a production machine) and radical 1970s smoked metalflake colour schemes.

In truth, the result wasn't either astonishingly fast, as fine handling as a Ducati or as luxurious as some. But as a combination of all three, as a 125mph sports-tourer with high-speed cruising ability, comfort, handling and BMW's traditional reliability and quality, the R90S was second to none.

The R90S's biggest strength was as a high-speed tourer as it proved adept at covering high mileages in luxurious comfort. (BMW)

WHAT THEY SAID

'Roads stream by under the flashing spokes, the exhaust is a civilised, subdued basso rumble. There's power to spare, reliability unquestioned, and only the omnipresent possibility of red lights twinkling in those big rear-view mirrors to keep you from giving the R90S its head.'

Cycle magazine, January 1974, on the $3965 BMW R90/S

Although the original 750 Commando was voted UK newspaper *MCN*'s 'Machine of the Year' five years in a row between 1968 and 1972, by the early 1970s Norton, along with the rest of the British motorcycle industry, was in big trouble. A larger 850, introduced in 1973 and featuring a number of updates, became the 'ultimate Commando' and arguably the most desirable British bike of the mid-1970s.

The original 750 Commando was famously created in under a year, born out of the collapse of Norton owners AMC in 1966. Norton, along with AJS and Matchless, were sold to Manganese Bronze, who owned Villiers. The new owners decided to focus on Norton, folding AJS and Matchless. The new company was renamed Norton-Villiers and its bosses tasked engineers Dr Stefan Bauer, John Favill, Bernard Hooper and Bob Trigg to come up with a new flagship Norton to be unveiled at the following year's Earl's Court Show.

The limited timescale meant retaining the 746cc, OHV, parallel-twin from the Norton Atlas but it was inclined forward to look more modern. Instead the new bike's defining feature was an all-new chassis, dubbed 'Isolastic', which isolated the engine's notorious vibrations, resulting in a bike that was adequately powerful (58bhp), fine handling and smooth. Its 'fastback' styling and Commando name weren't bad, either.

The original 750 Norton Commando had proved a big success, enough to be voted 'Machine of the Year' five years in a row. (Norton)

WHAT THEY SAID

'This new Commando would be my choice for the Machine of the Year if it wasn't for so many points of criticism over quality control.'

Motorcycle Mechanics magazine, June 1973, on the £726 Norton Commando 850

It was a success, too, prompting the addition of a US-aimed, scrambler-styled 'S' model in 1969; the Roadster in 1970; and a slightly bizarre cruiser variant, the Hi-Rider, in 1971. But 1972's Combat high-performance variant proved a disaster, prompting the 1973 introduction of the 828cc 850. It also saw the belated introduction of a disc front brake, while the 1975 Mk III also gained an electric starter and left-hand gearchange.

The 1975 Commandos were the most refined of all, but, sadly, it was also the last full year of production, with bikes from 1975 and 1976 basically built from surplus parts. It was an ignominious end to one of the greatest British bikes of all.

You can't accuse Norton for not trying! The British firm's advertising campaign for the new 850, featuring 'Norton Girls' such as, here, model Vivienne Neve, caused a sensation. (Norton)

WHO LOVED IT?

Like with the latest Triumph Bonneville, you had to be die-hard Brit bike fans to hand over your hard-earned for the 850 Commando. It wasn't a bad bike, but it had been outpaced by the Japanese and reliability concerns remained. Around 60,000 were built.

TRIUMPH X75 HURRICANE, 1973

The Trident-based X75 Hurricane was one of the boldest and most ambitiously styled bikes of the early 1970s. Sadly, even this wasn't enough to save Triumph. (Triumph)

Although by the mid-1970s Triumph, along with the rest of the British motorcycle industry, was in its final death throes, one of its last bikes was also one of its most striking and significant of all and is today among the most collectable British bikes – the 1973 X75 Hurricane.

And yet, in many ways, the Hurricane was neither a Triumph nor British at all, instead being conceived as a variant of the BSA Rocket3, born in the US and styled by Californian Craig Vetter.

Its story began with BSA/Triumph's unveiling of its new 750cc triples to American dealers in late 1968. Although new, the response to the Rocket3 and Trident was muted due to the bikes' controversial styling by Ogle, the firm which later designed the Raleigh Chopper.

Worse, soon afterwards Honda unveiled its all-new CB750, complete with an extra cylinder, more power, disc not drum brake, five (not four) gears, an electric (not kick) starter and tag of just $1,495, when the BSA was $1,795. Unsurprisingly, perhaps, US sales of the new Brit triples was slow.

WHAT THEY SAID

'Triumph have taken the plunge into a challenging new field and come up with what in the true sense of the word is the most exciting motorcycle built in Britain.'

Bike magazine, April 1973, on the £895 Triumph X75 Hurricane

The bold, one-piece tank/seat unit and triple side-mounted exhausts were designed by American Craig Vetter, initially for the BSA Rocket3. Today, the Hurricane is one of the most collectable of all 1970s bikes. (Triumph)

Don Brown, vice-president of BSA US, secretly commissioned stylist Vetter to create a restyled version. The result, with its stylised tank/seat and overlong front forks, was the Hurricane. After positive publicity in a number of US magazines, the prototype was shipped to England. But by the time it was put into production, BSA had already closed, which led to it instead becoming the Triumph X75.

In truth, it wasn't a commercial success. By then Triumph was in dire straits and it was still expensive, outdated and outpaced by the Japanese. But as a style icon and, today, a collector's piece, few motorcycles of the 1970s – and even fewer Triumphs – had as big an impact.

WHO LOVED IT?

Flamboyant and fabulous, the X75 was also too impractical, too Californian and, critically, too late to be a sales success, even in the US. Today, however, it remains one of the most desirable and valuable of all 1970s Triumphs. Just 1,172 were built.

2

JAPAN MAKES ITS 'MARQUES'

The 1976 Z650 was typical of the new breed of high-performance, multi-cylinder, affordable Japanese machines that would establish Kawasaki, alongside Suzuki, Yamaha and Honda, as the new brands to beat. (Kawasaki)

YAMAHA FS1-E, 1973

No bike of the early 1970s was as loved as much as Yamaha's FS1-E. The 50cc 'sixteener' arguably did more than any other to get a new generation onto two wheels for the first time. (Yamaha)

No small bike has been as significant or earned as big a place in the hearts of a biking generation as the Yamaha FS1-E.

Built specifically for England – it's a bespoke version of the FS1, hence the 'E' – the little Yamaha was one of the first machines produced in response to the UK's new 'sixteener' law introduced on 15 December 1971. Until then, 16-year-old learners could ride 250s, but this new restriction, intended to improve safety and reduce casualties, limited them to mopeds – two-wheelers defined as under 50cc with pedals which 'must be able to drive the machine'.

In response, Yamaha (and others) promptly came up with a series of 'sports 'peds' – slickly styled 50s capable of up to 55mph – that were anything but the sensible shopping mopeds legislators had envisaged. They became an overnight sensation.

Although Austrian maker Puch was first to market a sports 50, it was quickly followed by Yamaha's SS50 (for 'Sixteener Special') in 1972. This was then superseded by the mildly updated and renamed FS1-E in 1973, a 'be-pedalled' version of Yamaha's Europe-wide FS1.

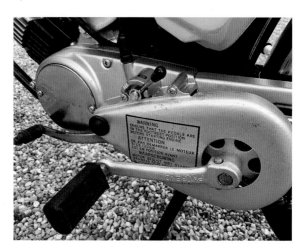

WHAT THEY SAID

'The FS1-E is Yamaha's reigning best-seller and our favourite. It has the looks of an exciting lightweight and that tireless two-stroke motor delivers the performance to match.'

Bike magazine, March 1975, on the £215 Yamaha FS1-E

Ugly, maybe, but the FS1-E's moped pedals were crucial for Yamaha's 50mph 'sports 'ped' to comply with the UK's new 'sixteener' learner law, which came into force in 1971. (Yamaha)

The FS1-E was initially launched as the SS50, for 'Sixteener Special' – note the 'SS' badge on this early example's side panels. (Yamaha)

And, with a simple, disc-valve, two-stroke single producing 4.8bhp, pressed steel frame, great styling (initially in Popsicle Purple or Candy Orange) and idiot-proof durability, the FS1-E became a massive hit.

Although rivals produced capable alternatives – most notably Honda with its four-stroke SS50, Suzuki with its AP50, plus European offerings from the likes of Gilera, Garelli, Fantic and Casal – it was the 'Fizzy' that became the must-have machine, propelling a generation of 16-year-olds between chip shops in a plume of blue smoke. In 1974 the Yamaha was also available in Baja Brown, and in 1976, it gained a disc front brake and 'speed block' graphics, later becoming a cult machine.

It couldn't last, of course. Tabloid scare stories of teenage moped gangs helped prompt a further change in the learner law and, from 1 August 1977, mopeds were restricted to 30mph. The 'sport-ped' era was over.

Decades later, however, middle-aged men, nostalgic for their misspent youth, began restoring now-classic Fizzies, making it one of the most in-demand 50s in history, with prices often well in excess of £5,000.

No, they don't look 16, do they? In fact the models in this promotional picture are Finnish Yamaha factory rider Jarno Saarinen and his wife Soili. (Yamaha)

WHO LOVED IT?

From early 1972, any British 16-year-old interested in two wheels would have traded their Oxford bags in an instant for a 'Fizzy'. It was a huge hit, selling 7,500 in its first year with an average 15,000 annually over the next three years.

YAMAHA RD250/400, 1973

Yamaha's hooligan two-stroke RD250/400 twins were the must-have lightweight sportsters of the mid-1970s. This is a later 'D' model in GP star Kenny Roberts replica yellow and black. (Yamaha)

No Japanese manufacturer is more closely associated with the twin-cylinder sports stroker than Yamaha. And throughout the 1970s, no Yamaha was more popular than the brilliant RD250 and 400 duo.

Yamaha has been associated with two-stroke 250 twins from its earliest days in the 1950s. Founded in 1955, Yamaha first hit the track in 1958 with its YD1 twin, and became world champions in 1964 and 1965. A 350 roadster followed in 1967 and by 1971, its YDS7 250 with 30bhp was the performance benchmark with both rebranded as 'RD's (Race Developed) in 1973.

The most fondly remembered versions, however, debuted following an angular restyle for 1976 when the 350 also became a 400. With distinctive, square, 'coffin-shaped' tanks, and 'speed block' striping, both now had the wild looks to match their screaming performance, enough for them to become the aspirational poster bikes for a generation of '70s bikers.

WHO LOVED IT?

Any self-respecting 1970s street – or track (where it cleaned up in production racing) – racer. Exact production numbers of the RD250 are not known, but around 38,000 400s were built.

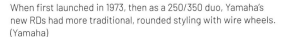

When first launched in 1973, then as a 250/350 duo, Yamaha's new RDs had more traditional, rounded styling with wire wheels. (Yamaha)

The final 1979 'F' version was the best of all, but by then it had been overtaken by Suzuki's new lightweight X7. The all-new RD250LC would reclaim Yamaha's No. 1 spot in 1980. (Yamaha)

The first RD250C had wire wheels and 30bhp, while the RD400 had wires, a rear disc brake and 10bhp more. Handling wasn't brilliant, but it was sufficient for both to be the speediest bikes in their class. Then things got better still: 1977's RD250D had seven spoke alloys, new rear bodywork and a bold new yellow/black colour option; the 1978 RD250E got CDI ignition, revised porting and exhausts and was available in Yamaha racing white/red; while the 1979 RD250F gained dog-leg levers and was promoted by new world champion Kenny Roberts.

But it was the end of the line. Suzuki's lightweight 1978 GT250X7 prompted a rethink that resulted in the all-new, liquid-cooled RD250/350LC duo that kicked off the 1980s. But for most of the 1970s, the air-cooled RD was stroker king.

WHAT THEY SAID

'The Yamaha really has to be pick of the performance-orientated 400s, and not only because of its dynamic motor, at £625 (or £675 for the cast wheel version) the RD is also devastatingly competitive on price.'

Bike magazine, August 1976, on the £625 Yamaha RD400C

NORTON COMMANDO 850 JPS REPLICA, 1974

The 'John Player Replica' was a limited edition road bike built to capitalize on Norton's early 1970s success with its novel-looking, cigarette-firm-backed racers. (Norton)

Although the 1970s saw the decline of the once great British motorcycle industry, there were still some hallelujah moments. One of the greatest was the brief brilliance of the John Player Norton racing team between 1972 and 1974, as commemorated by the road replica: the Norton Commando 850 JPS Replica.

Following the race team's success in both the 1973 TT and British superbike championships (see opposite page), the Norton factory, desperate for a sales 'winner' too, built a limited edition, road-going replica.

WHAT THEY SAID

'The Norton 850 is an elitist's motorcycle and the John Player Special is the most elite Norton of all. It's the namesake of the Norton factory race bikes ... but it's not a production racer-replica of anything, the Player bike is a standard Commando dressed up in race-track clothes.'

Cycle magazine, 1974, on the $2,995 Norton Commando JPS

THE JOHN PLAYER NORTON RACER

The Formula 750 motorcycle racing class introduced in the early 1970s has a lot to answer for. The production-based series launched in the US in 1971, in world championships in 1972 and in the UK in 1973 and prompted not only the creation of the Rob North-framed 'Beezumph' BSA/Triumph triples, which won the 1971 Daytona 200 and spawned the first Anglo-American Match Races soon after, but also prompted Dennis Poore, Norton chairman, to commission a one-off F750 prototype based on the 750 Commando.

The John Player Norton racer was developed by brilliant rider/engineer Peter Williams. (Norton)

The bike was developed by factory racer and development engineer Peter Williams, who compensated for the Norton's lack of power with aerodynamics and superior handling.

With sponsorship from John Player, the first blue-liveried bikes, ridden mostly by Williams and Phil Read, showed promise. But in 1973, an all-new monocoque chassis proved a revelation and, with new bodywork in striking white/red and blue livery and a rider line-up of Williams and Dave Croxford in equally striking white leathers, the JPS Norton dominated British racing. Williams won the F750 TT, three rounds of the Transatlantic Trophy and placed second in the MCN superbike championship, while Croxford won the British 750cc series.

Then 1974 saw the team switch to a more conventional chassis with less success, with Williams suffering a career-ending crash. Cash-strapped, the team was disbanded at the end of the year. But the glories of 1973 ensured the JPS Norton's legend would be etched into history.

The road replica, although essentially only a rebodied Commando and not a great sales success at the time, today remains one of the most iconic of British 1970s classics. (Norton)

With limited funds, the result was little more than a lookalike: a standard Mk2A Commando 850 with facsimile bodywork comprising a one-piece fairing/tank cover made by Avon with matching single seat in replica white/red/blue race livery. Performance of the aging pushrod twin was unchanged at 60bhp, there was still just a four-speed gearbox and single Lockheed disc brake, tank capacity was miserly and, for taller riders, it was uncomfortable too.

But the Replica was arguably the raciest British bike yet built. It also looked easily worth its $500 premium over the standard bike and proved a big hit.

Modern bikers often refer to Suzuki's 1985 GSX-R750F as the first 'racer replica'. Not a bit of it. Norton got there first in the 1970s. And then some.

WHO LOVED IT?

A total of 200 were built and all sold out, with most (120) going to the US. Today it remains one of the most collectable of all British bikes of the 1970s.

RICKMAN CR, 1974

While the new Japanese superbikes of the early 1970s raised the bar for road-bike performance, the same certainly wasn't true of handling – quite the opposite. Although Honda's CB750 outpaced all comers with 67bhp and Kawasaki's Z1 900 of 1972 raised the bar further with 82bhp, both were heavy with chassis that struggled to cope.

This is where specialist European frame builders such as Egli, Moto Martin and, later, Bimota came in.

In Britain, one of the most successful were the Rickman brothers. Derek and Don Rickman made their name in the 1960s with their Metisse scrambler kits, creating one of the most successful off-roaders of the decade and famously finding favour with Hollywood icon and bike nut Steve McQueen.

Then in the early 1970s, as road motorcycling shifted towards the new four-cylinder Japanese machines, Rickman turned their attention to frames – and indeed whole kits including sports fairing, tank, seat and more – first for Honda's CB and then Kawasaki's Z1.

The result, the Rickman CR, was one of the sexiest, best handling and fastest motorcycles of the 1970s. The only trouble was: you had to build it yourself, using your own bike as donor of engine, clocks, lights and more.

With their nickel-plated frames, gorgeous fibreglass (the donor bikes' side panels were retained) and top-quality cycle parts including Borrani rims and Lockheed brakes, the CR not only looked fabulous, it moved even better. Unfortunately, it cost $1,495 (on top of the donor bike), had to be self-built and had a cramped riding position, keeping them the preserve of an exclusive few. Worse, Rickman's reign was short-lived with the company halting production of complete bikes in the mid-1970s to concentrate on accessories. But for a glorious couple of years, a Rickman CR 900 was simply the ultimate.

Good-looking, fine-handling and fast, a Rickman CR based on the Kawasaki Z1 engine was among the ultimate of all mid-1970s superbikes. (Rickman)

WHAT THEY SAID

'The chassis is rigidly accurate and the brakes perfect ... and the looks this beauty gets ... even old ladies in their Caddies do a double take. You can imagine the conversation inside the last cop car you encountered. "Hey Herkewicz, that guy's got a racing bike on the street."'

Cycle World magazine, July 1974, on the $1,495 Rickman CR Honda CB750

WHO LOVED IT?

The ultimate 'British' sports bike of the mid-1970s, the CR was also expensive, exclusive and the preserve of those with mechanical know-how. Production numbers aren't known but were minimal.

HONDA CB400F, 1974

Honda's four-cylinder CB400F opened the door of multi-cylinder motorcycling to a whole new generation. (Honda)

While the CB750, launched in 1969, is rightly celebrated as the first mainstream four-cylinder superbike, it is Honda's smaller spin-off, launched in 1974, that was even more significant in introducing a whole generation to affordable Japanese four-cylinder fun – the CB400F.

Unveiled at the Cologne show in the autumn of 1974, the '400 Four', as it's more commonly known, was much more than just a junior CB750. Styled specifically for Europe with a sinuous

four-into-one sports exhaust that remains an icon to this day, the 400/4 also handled well and had a 'proper' big bike specification including disc front brake and six-speed gearbox. The latter, when used vigorously in conjunction with its 37bhp, delivered enough performance to hang onto the coat tails of rival two-strokes such as the KH350 and Suzuki GT380 – but with far more style.

Smaller, lighter and, crucially, cheaper than then 750 or 900cc four-cylinder bikes, the CB400F proved a big hit in the UK. (Honda)

The CB400F looked good and went well – performing on a par with most two-stroke twins of the era. Sadly, however, it didn't sell well in the US and it was dropped after just two years. (Honda)

As such, the CB400F was the first true 'mini superbike' and as it cost £669 when launched (two-thirds the price of a CB750), it was one that was within reach of a new generation of 1970s sports bike enthusiasts brought up on tales of Mike Hailwood's Honda 'Six' and 'Ago' and Phil Read's MVs.

And yet Honda's 'junior jewel' was not a commercial success. Although popular in the UK, it was expensive to produce and it never took off in the important US market, meaning it was withdrawn from production after only two years.

Sporty CB400/4-specific features included a striking and sinuous four-into-one exhaust and novel six-speed gearbox. (Honda)

WHO LOVED IT?

Japanese superbike-savvy youngsters who only had student budgets – particularly in the UK which proved its biggest market. However, despite over 100,000 sold, poor sales in the US led to it being dropped after just two years.

Today, however, the CB400/4 is viewed very differently. As a 'mini CB750' it's as much a technical marvel as its bigger brother. As an object of '70s lust it's a time machine back to fifty-somethings' youth. As an affordable Honda with plenty of examples still available (plus the spares back-up to match) it's a great 'starter classic' for those for whom a CB750 or Z1 are simply out of financial reach.

SUZUKI RE-5, 1974

The radical, rotary-powered RE-5 was Suzuki's 'great white hope' of the mid-1970s. Instead, it turned out to be an expensive white elephant. (Suzuki)

The RE-5 was one of the most astounding motorcycles of the 1970s: one of the most ambitious, one of the most advanced but ultimately also one of the most disastrous, jeopardising the whole Suzuki company. And it all boils down to one word: Wankel.

Through much of the 1960s the innovative rotary engine, as developed by Felix Wankel for Germany's NSU car company, was viewed almost as automotive's holy grail for its light weight and creamy power, attributes that also favoured use in motorcycles.

In 1970 Suzuki, keen to move into big bikes after its stroker lightweights but also wanting to set itself apart from Honda's (and later Kawasaki's) four-stroke fours, bought a licence from NSU and promptly set up a development programme for its new flagship. It even employed Italian car designer Giorgetto Giugiaro for styling, which included a whacky 'barrel' instrument pod and tail light. The result, four long years later, was the RE-5.

WHAT THEY SAID

'The Suzuki gives you a lot of very complex machinery for your money, which is OK if you want complexity and technical sophistication for its own sake; but when you realize you can buy a GT750 for £300 less, or the performance of a Kawasaki Z1 for around the same price, it perhaps doesn't seem so good.'

Bike magazine, November 1975, on the £1195 Suzuki RE-5

First press reports were positive and journalists raved about its smooth power, decent handling and style. But soon, concerns started to surface. With the fuel crisis dominating the news, the RE-5's high fuel consumption of 35–37mpg suddenly rang alarm bells. Its hefty weight also became an issue, while the rotary's performance, with a top speed of just 110mph, was no better than Suzuki's own GT750 (which cost £300 less).

All of that, combined with a few rotor failures, resulted in a sales disaster not aided by a revised design with conventional clocks and tail light for 1975. Suzuki then abandoned the whole project after less than two years, turning instead to its new series of GS four-strokes.

The RE-5 itself wasn't as bad as stories suggest. It was cruelly tainted by the mid-1970s oil crisis and was a bold project that, with perhaps a little more development, might have paid off. Instead, the RE-5 remains the only mass-production rotary motorcycle in history and a 1970s motorcycling milestone.

A hasty restyle provided more conventional instruments and improved its looks, but couldn't mask the RE-5's underwhelming performance and excessive cost. (Suzuki)

WHO LOVED IT?

Suzuki fans, early adopters and ... not many others. Although interesting and effective, the RE-5 was also underwhelming, expensive and short-lived. By the end of its production life, just 6,500 RE-5s had been produced.

Despite impressively smooth running, a fanfare launch and generally good early press reports, the RE-5 ultimately proved a costly disaster for Suzuki that nearly sank the whole company. (Suzuki)

Honda followed up its revolutionary CB750 with the even bigger, and arguably even more innovative, GL1000 Gold Wing. A first, the motorcycling world didn't know what to make of it ... (Honda)

Few bikes create such a following you need only refer to them only by their model name. But in the mid-1970s, a machine was launched that did just that and in due course changed motorcycling forever: the Gold Wing.

Unveiled in 1974, the Wing quickly grew and evolved to define the full-dress touring motorcycle. The 1980 GL1100 Interstate introduced full fairings and panniers. It grew to 1,200cc in 1984, then 1,500cc and six cylinders in 1988, while the modern GL1800 epitomises motorcycling luxury.

The first GL1000 was conceived as a successor to Honda's own CB750. In 1972, Soichiro Honda was irked by both the CB's overshadowing by the Z1 900 from Kawasaki, and also by Harley-Davidson and BMW's continued dominance of the American touring market.

In response, he tasked a project team to explore what form the largest, fastest and best touring machine might take. The prototype they came up with was dubbed the M1 and featured a mammoth 1,470cc, liquid-cooled flat six, shaft drive and twin discs.

Among the features of Honda's new leviathan was liquid-cooling – the first Honda road bike so equipped. To help keep its centre of gravity low, the fuel tank was also under the seat. (Honda)

WHAT THEY SAID

'The GL1000 is a prestige machine and a winner ... despite its few unfortunate shortcomings. It's nimble for its weight, smooth as good Scotch and as quiet as time passing. It may soon be THE touring machine on American highways.'

Cycle World magazine, April 1975, on the c. $3,000 Honda GL1000

Although considered too extreme, the M1 paved the way for what was to follow and, with the engine required to be larger than the 903cc Z1, a shorter, four-cylinder, 999cc version was settled upon. And although many of the M1's other innovations, such as fuel injection and anti-lock brakes, were also rejected, the resulting GL1000 Gold Wing – its name taken from Honda's company emblem – still made a massive impression when officially unveiled in Cologne.

In truth, it wasn't an immediate success. In Europe its weight and liquid-cooled engine led to 'two-wheeled car' criticisms. In the US, its lack of weather protection and luggage meant buyers were slow to realise its touring potential.

But fortunes improved slowly, particularly in the US when aftermarket factory fairings and luggage became available. As a result, by turn of the decade, when the GL1100 arrived, a dominant, full-dress dynasty was well underway.

Although not an immediate sales success, the Gold Wing eventually established itself as a touring 'tour de force' and, fitted with fairing and luggage, became the benchmark 'full dress tourer'. (Honda)

WHO LOVED IT?

Although not the immediate success hoped for – instead of the projected 60,000 sales, just 5,000 examples were sold in the first year – the Gold Wing evolved into one of Honda's biggest success stories, defining the 'full-dress tourer' and gaining a huge following, plus its own production plant in the US. Now 1,800cc, over 640,000 have so far been built.

MOTO MORINI 3½ SPORT, 1974

Like other exotic, expensive Italian motorcycles of the 1970s, the Morini 3½ Sport was a fantasy for most bikers and a reality only for an exclusive, well-heeled few.

Dating back to 1937, Moto Morini had made its name in lightweight, sporting four-stroke singles. In 1971, it unveiled its first 72-degree V-twin prototype in 350cc form, chosen due to the heavy Italian taxes then levied on machines over this capacity.

The Moto Morini 3½ Sport may, in the mid-1970s, have seemed slightly old-fashioned and expensive, but in every other respect it was true Italian exotica in a mini 350cc package. (Moto Morini)

Later examples had more modern styling with more extensive bodywork, disc brakes and cast wheels. (Moto Morini)

WHO LOVED IT?

Expensive to buy and hard to find, in the 1970s Morinis were the preserve of well-heeled, devoted, Italian connoisseurs. Between 1973 and 1986 Morini produced 2–3,000 bikes a year, with around two-thirds of those 350s.

Early examples came with curvy styling, quality Grimeca drum brakes and wire wheels. They remain the most desirable to collectors today. (Moto Morini)

Produced first in 35bhp GT form, the Sport followed in 1974, with an extra 4bhp thanks to a rise in compression and sportier cam. Thanks also to its clip-ons, race seat and alloy Borrani rims incorporating a larger Grimeca drum front brake, it immediately became the most lusted-after model.

The tubular steel frame and Ceriani rear and Marzocchi front suspension delivered handling among the best anywhere, it was great looking and it was every inch junior Italian exotica.

In the UK, however, it cost around £350 more than Yamaha's similarly powerful two-stroke RD350. Also, the Morini's finish and spec seemed dated, with crude switchgear and clocks, and, like other Italian machines of the era, reliability wasn't great, which all conspired to result in few takers.

For 1976 it gained a disc front brake with a double-disc option, and from 1978 alloy wheels and an electric starter made an appearance. The bike lived on into the mid-1980s with further styling and detail changes, none being a huge success.

In more recent years Morini's 'mini jewel' has become revered as an affordable, usable Italian classic with early models fetching the best prices – a slightly ironic fact, as it was never that much of a success at the time.

WHAT THEY SAID

'The Moto Morini 3½ Sport is expensive, demanding and impractical. What you get for your money and emotional involvement is a motorcycle that moves you and makes you feel good. For the lucky few, the Morini is worth what it costs.'

Cycle World magazine, April 1977, on the $2,100 Moto Morini 3½ Sport

YAMAHA TY50/80, 1975

Looking back from the luxury of the twenty-first century, it's easy to forget the huge popularity of trials in the 1970s, when *Kickstart* was on primetime BBC1; Spanish brands like Bultaco, Montesa and OSSA ruled the 'off-road, feet-up' roost; and great British riders such as Mick Andrews, Martin Lampkin and Malcolm Rathmell were consecutive world champions.

The recipe for a successful trials machine back then was a lightweight but punchy air-cooled, single cylinder, two-stroke engine, a simple twin shock, tubular-steel chassis and a world-leading rider to develop it, as Bultaco had done in hiring Sammy Miller and OSSA with Andrews in the 1960s.

In the early 1970s, however, Yamaha decided it wanted a slice of the action and hired Andrews in 1973 to develop its own version. That bike was the TY250 (with TY standing for 'Trial Yamaha'), on which Andrews himself went on to win two more Scottish Six Days Trials in 1974 and 1975. But the Buxton native also went on to design further spin-offs for Yamaha: the 'midi' TY175 and

WHAT THEY SAID

'The TY80A is a very curious "trailer". It's a machin that lacks proper trials bike geometry and has rathe marginal traction, but it's a bike capable of doing well i trials events and is an absolute ball to ride. It will com as no surprise to us if Yamaha dealers sell every TY8 they can get their hands on.'

Cycle World magazine, March 1974, on the $386 Yamaha T

The 'mini' TY was an almost inch-perfect – but 80 per cent scale – replica of Yamaha's new full-sized trials machines that had been developed by Brit Mick Andrews. (Yamaha)

Both were hugely popular and remained in production over a number of variants throughout the late 1970s. Today they're cherished as easy, affordable and cute modern classics. (Yamaha)

The mini TY's bigger brothers, meanwhile, available in 125, 175 and 250cc forms, were also hugely popular and successful. (Yamaha)

TY125, and two even smaller, cuter 'mini-trial' versions, the TY50 and 80, on which so many future world champions would gain their first taste of trials.

The genius of the TY50 and 80 was that they were in no way 'toy' motorcycles, but instead proper, scaled-down trials machines albeit with a slightly simplified four-or-five-speed gearchange. Better still, a number of variants were produced over its lifetime with different wheel sizes, gears, lights etc., and as they were built to the same high standards as Yamaha's full-size machines and were durable and simple to work on, they were top of the Christmas list of any bike-mad '70s youngster. Today they remain popular as easy and affordable restoration projects, and as cute, classic reminders of a generation of bikers' youth.

WHO LOVED IT?

Although Spanish Montesa and others also built junior trials bikes in the 1970s, the Yamaha TY50 and TY80 were far and away the most desirable youth off-roaders of the era. They remain cherished today among fifty-somethings keen to revisit their youth.

YAMAHA TT/XT500, 1975

In the mid-1970s Yamaha was also busy, not just with 'trial' bikes, but also with trail bikes: its all new, big-bore XT500 would lead a trend towards ever-bigger off-road machines. (Yamaha)

Today, being familiar with enormous 1,300cc, multi-cylinder adventure bikes, it's hard to imagine a time when a 500cc four-stroke trail bike was revolutionary – but that's exactly what Yamaha's 1975 XT500 was in the mid-1970s.

Launched at a time when lightweight two-stroke 'trailies' were all the rage and big 'thumpers' were deemed old fashioned, the XT (plus its sister enduro version, the TT) was developed in response to the American market's demand for ever-bigger, more reliable 'desert sleds', and also because the Japanese firm was keen to expand its four-stroke range after previously being dependent on 'strokers'.

Although a big 500cc, four-stroke machine, Yamaha went to great lengths to keep its all-new XT as slim and light as possible by using, for example, aluminium for its fuel tank instead of conventional steel. (Yamaha)

WHAT THEY SAID

'Let's face it, the XT is breaking new ground, whether as a competition machine or as a road bike.'

Motorcycle Monthly magazine, November 1976, on the £685 Yamaha XT500

In an attempt to avoid the criticisms of previous big singles, Yamaha made the new bike as light and slim as possible. Thus, the TT had magnesium crankcase covers and both versions had aluminium tanks. An all-new frame, meanwhile, featured an integral oil tank for the first time on a Japanese machine.

The TT came first in 1975, with the street-legal XT following in 1976. Both were instant hits in the US, inspiring a series of rivals. Honda's XL500 arrived in 1979, Suzuki's DR500 in 1980 and Kawasaki's KLR600 in 1984, together launching a new era of 'monster trailies'.

More surprising was the XT500's success in Europe. The new Yamaha was perfectly suited to endurance off-road events and, after coming first and second in the inaugural Paris-Dakar Rally in 1979, then taking the top four places in 1980, the big Yamaha spawned a dynasty of XTs and Ténéré adventure variants that prove popular to this day.

WHO LOVED IT?

Although it remained fairly niche in the UK, the XT was hugely popular in the US and in Europe, particularly France and Italy. It went out of production in 1981, replaced first by the XT550, then XT600.

The XT500 proved especially popular in Continental Europe, particularly in Italy and France, and went on to dominate the first Paris-Dakar Rally in 1979. (Yamaha)

MOTO GUZZI 850 T3 CALIFORNIA, 1975

By 1975, Moto Guzzi's 850cc twins were already a success but the T3, with its pioneering linked brakes and other refinements, became the definitive example, particularly in touring California style. (Moto Guzzi)

Although Italian manufacturer Moto Guzzi dates back to 1921, and its signature transverse V-twin layout first found success with the V7 and 1971's V7 Sport, the most famous and lusted-after Guzzis of the decade came a little later – the T3 850-based Le Mans sportster and the touring California.

Both came in 1975 as developments of the 850 T of 1971. Guzzi chief engineer Lino Tonti had re-engineered Guzzi's V-twin from a heavy tourer into a more sporting 844cc machine. By moving the alternator to the front of the engine, the riding position could be lowered along with the centre of gravity, while using the engine as a stressed member improved its already impressive rigidity. In 1975 the '3' bit, meanwhile, indicated the debut of Guzzi's innovative triple-disc linked brake system, whereby the brake pedal operated rear and right front caliper, with the handlebar lever operating the left.

WHAT THEY SAID

'It's the ancillaries that usually let Italian bikes down. So it was with the California. But I wouldn't let such niggles put me off this grand bike, not for a moment. I kept my claws on it for as long as I decently could and I still bore the staff by rambling about its virtues.'

Motorcycling Monthly magazine, October 1976, on the £1,599 Moto Guzzi 850 T3 California

The T3 California was the updated version of the US-style tourer that first debuted in 1971. That first 750cc machine was co-developed with the Los Angeles Police Department as a patrol bike, hence its big black and white solo seat, screen, panniers and footboards, and it proved popular with many US police forces, including the California Highway Patrol (CHiPs).

So named for being derived from a patrol version developed for the West Coast police, the California was Europe's best and most recognisable tourer of the mid-1970s. (Moto Guzzi)

With its hard panniers, high Plexiglas screen and sumptuous, deeply padded and distinctive black and white seat, the T3 California quickly became a 1970s icon. (Moto Guzzi)

A civilian version then followed named California, which was also a big hit. But it was in T3 form that the California proved most popular for its classic monochrome styling, comfort, easy handling and Harley-beating performance, so much so that it established the model as an ever-present in Guzzi's line-up right up to 2020.

WHO LOVED IT?

Fans of Guzzi and American-style tourers who wanted Italian handling, braking and style. The T3 was the most-loved Guzzi of the 1970s, with the California its most famous incarnation.

BMW R100RS, 1976

No European superbike of the mid-1970s looked more futuristic, fast or flash than BMW's revolutionary, fully faired R100RS – even TV's *The Saint* had one! (BMW)

Developed in Pininfarina's wind tunnel and styled by Hans Muth (who'd earlier styled the R90S), the R100RS's aerodynamic fairing was both effective and utterly distinctive. (BMW)

The traditional boxer engine was BMW's largest and most powerful yet and, combined with the RS's wind-cheating abilities, was enough to give the RS a top speed of around 125mph. (BMW)

One of the most dramatic-looking, desirable – and expensive – motorcycles of the mid-1970s actually came from one of the least likely sources: BMW.

The Bavarian firm's new 1976 flagship R100RS was radical not for being the biggest boxer twin yet, or the most powerful (both of which it was, at 980cc and 70bhp respectively, having grown from the 898cc and 67bhp of 1973's R90S) but for being one of the first bikes designed to have a full fairing.

And what a fairing it was! Styled by in-house designer Hans Muth and optimised aerodynamically in Pininfarina's wind tunnel, the RS's striking fibreglass combined with the bigger engine to make the new bike BMW's fastest ever at 125mph. What's more, slathered in metallic silver and equipped with BMW's new 'snowflake' alloy wheels, the RS was also one of the most stylish and modern-looking bikes of the era.

In truth, underneath the plastic and bigger numbers the RS wasn't that remarkable. Yes, the engine was bigger, the chassis stronger and the bodywork mostly new, but the RS was still essentially a sober, sensible and expensive tourer rather than any kind of sports powerhouse. Even so, for covering vast distances at speed there was little better. As a status symbol nothing came close, and as a poster bike and Top Trumps winner the RS was up there with the best. No fairing since is as recognisable as that of the R100RS.

As well as cast wheels, the RS was also offered with an optional '3/4' single seat, which enhanced the big BMW's aerodynamic looks even more. (BMW)

WHO LOVED IT?

Futuristic, effective and exclusively expensive, the R100RS was the ultimate 'gentleman's express' for those wanting the best in long-range luxury. It remained in production until 1984 by which time 33,648 had been built.

MOTO GUZZI LE MANS MKI, 1976

While Moto Guzzi's T3 850 California established a new standard for Italian touring machines in the 1970s, the company's 850 Le Mans, based on the same engine and chassis, set a new flavour for Italian sportsters.

Conceived as a successor to the brilliant V7 Sport, the new bike was inspired by Guzzi's endurance racing campaign with a modified V7 Sport in 1971. Enlarged to 844cc, the racer led the Bol d'Or 24-hour race, then led Le Mans for ten hours before finishing third, hence the name.

For the road version, Guzzi took the road 850 T's 844cc engine, tuned it with high-compression pistons, new cams and bigger 36mm Dell'Orto carbs, boosting power to 81bhp, and employed the new T3 linked brakes with Brembo calipers and drilled discs.

The Le Mans used a tuned version of the latest 850 V-twin, gave it top-spec cycle parts, a racy riding position including single seat and dressed it all in aggressive new bodywork, including a stylish small headlamp fairing. (Moto Guzzi)

WHAT THEY SAID

'Twisty roads are what the Le Mans was designed for and twisty roads are where it sparkles. The Guzzi's geometry and wheelbase are such that the bike has a responsiveness missing in the big Ducatis and a feeling of solidity that over the years has been refined out of the Laverda 1000.'

Cycle magazine, August 1977, on the
$3,679 Moto Guzzi 850 Le Mans

Magazine road tests of the time fawned over the new Le Mans, not least *Cycle* magazine in the US, who rated it ahead of the latest Ducatis and Laverdas. (Author's collection)

To give it proper sports-bike attitude, it was given clip-on handlebars, rear-set footrests and a humped seat. And to give it the style to match, it had a saucy small flyscreen and brazen livery either in racing red or metallic blue.

The result, while not quite as fast as the latest multis from Japan, was still capable of 125mph, could see off all European rivals bar the best from Ducati and Laverda, had fabulous planted, lazy handling and sounded like nothing else. In short: the Le Mans looked great, went well, handled better and had a bellowing soundtrack little outside Italy could match. No wonder it was so desirable.

WHO LOVED IT?

The Le Mans' lazy style, character and sound proved such a hit the bike became a mainstay of Guzzi's range, living on through five 'marks' into the 1990s and growing to 1,000cc. None, however, are as much loved – or as valuable today – as that 1976 original.

LAVERDA JOTA, 1976

In the mid-1970s no big sports bike looked as fast and menacing – even at standstill – than Italian legend Laverda's astonishing Jota 1000. (Laverda)

No bike of the 1970s had as brutal a performance reputation as Laverda's legendary Jota 1000. Launched in 1976, the big, burly, three-cylinder Italian monster was effectively a special, British-built performance version of an already beastly machine – Laverda's 3C. Most importantly, when the UK's *Motor Cycle Weekly* newspaper tested it at the MIRA proving ground, the orange beast posted a best one-way top speed of 140.04mph when Kawasaki's 'king' Z1 900 was capable of 'just' 131. A new speed king had arrived. The following year it gained a name, that of an Italian dance in triple time – Jota.

Although based on the 981cc 3C triple launched in 1973, the Jota was the brainchild of UK Laverda importers Slater Brothers who decided to produce a performance version in order to grab glory in the then nascent Avon Roadrunner production bike race series. By 1975, Laverda already offered a 3C-E version (English version) with a performance exhaust, which raised power from 68 to 75bhp plus twin Brembo disc brakes, but the Slaters went further still. The bike that became the Jota then gained performance cams, altered carburation taking power to 90bhp, a race seat, disc rear brake and five-spoke cast alloys. Racers, meanwhile, could also get a close-ratio gearbox.

Named after an Italian dance, the Jota was actually a UK creation – a performance version of the existing 3C triple that was primarily intended to win on track and test strip. (Laverda)

WHAT THEY SAID

'The new Jota is everything an Italian motorcycle is supposed to be. It's fast. It's flashy. It's expensive. It's uncompromisingly sporting. And, above all, it's exclusive.'

Cycle Guide, June 1977, on the $4,495 Laverda Jota

Although the Jota's reign was relatively short and few bikes were built, the big orange triple remains one of the most iconic of all 1970s performance motorcycles. (Laverda)

In reality, of course, the Jota was an uncompromising, intimidating beast. Handling wasn't bad but it was tall, top-heavy with a heavy clutch and had a high first gear, irritating switchgear, erratic electrics and extreme riding position – all the things that separate 'pure' racers from civilised road bikes. But as a symbolic performance king, no 1970s machine did it better than the immense, handsome, bright orange 'Beast from Breganze'.

WHO LOVED IT?

The beastly, bristly Jota was simply the biggest and fastest bike of the mid-1970s, even if it was also impractical and expensive. Being a 'special', with many replicas also built, means exact production numbers are uncertain, but just 7,100 Laverda 1000s of all types were built in total.

KAWASAKI Z650, 1976

Just when 1970s bikers were beginning to think Kawasaki's 1972 Z1 900 was a one-off, the Japanese giant shocked the motorcycling world once again with the 1976 Z650.

Designed by the same genius behind the Z1, Gyoichi 'Ben' Inamura, the Z650 was another all-new, air-cooled, DOHC, transverse-four but this time a middleweight aimed at a more mainstream market.

WHAT THEY SAID

'It's competitively priced and represents excellent value as a quick and manageable sports/tourer – but therein lies the problem. Because the Kawasaki is intended to mean many things to many bikers it's the one most likely to be dismissed as "just another Japanese four".'

Bike magazine, March 1977, on the £1,075 Kawasaki Z650

And once again Kawasaki chose to do things differently. While the Z1 was a 903cc machine launched into a world where 750cc had been the multi-cylinder norm, its new little brother was a 650 when rivals from Honda and Suzuki were 550. The idea was to produce a four-cylinder that was not so big and heavy as to be intimidating and inaccessible but still have the character of a sporting multi. By achieving just that with a decent 64bhp yet a dry weight of just 465lb, Kawasaki kickstarted a new 650 class which Yamaha, Honda and more would soon follow.

As such, the Z650 was arguably even more important than the Z1. It was more innovative, technically, in using plain crank bearings in place of the Z1's rollers, a Hy-Vo chain between crank and transmission instead of the Z1's gears and as a result was both smoother and less expensive to make.

And although never as much of a 'poster bike' or as 'sexy' as the Z1 (despite the use of bikini-clad models at its UK launch), the 650 was commercially more significant in forming the basis of nearly all four-cylinder Kawasakis for the next decade. Without the Z650, 1970s motorcycling simply wouldn't have been the same.

The press launch took place in Scotland with some typically 1970s 'dolly birds' to hand. The Z650 went on to become one of Kawasaki's longest-living and most popular machines. (Kawasaki)

Although not as bold, brash or fast as the Z1, the Z650 was more affordable and versatile and established itself as a true Japanese multi-cylinder motorcycle for the masses. (Kawasaki)

WHO LOVED IT?

As with Honda's CB400F and Suzuki's GS550, the Z650 quickly established itself as a midi four-cylinder superbike for the masses. It was hugely popular and its engine lived on right up to the mid-1990s in Kawasaki's 750 Zephyr.

SUZUKI GS750, 1976

After the rotary-powered RE-5 debacle, Suzuki desperately needed a four-stroke, four-cylinder, mass-market success story. They got exactly that – and more – with the 1976 GS750. (Suzuki)

Up to the mid 1970s, Suzuki was associated almost exclusively with two-strokes such as the GT550 and GT750 'kettle' and dirt bikes, but with the fuel crisis looming and impending tighter emissions regulations, particularly in the US, things clearly had to change. The Japanese firm's prime focus was on its radical, rotary RE-5 that launched in 1974, which would prove a short-lived disaster that almost broke the company. Luckily, however, it hadn't put all its eggs in one basket. Following the lead of Honda and Kawasaki, Suzuki had also been quietly developing a far more conservative air-cooled, four-stroke, 750cc DOHC two-valve four and, after secretly testing it in the US in 1975, the result was launched in mid-1976.

The GS750 had to succeed – and it did. Although conservative to the point of drawing criticism that it was actually copied from Kawasaki (it did have the same valve timing, angles and valve sizes as the Z1 900), it was more refined, lighter and with a far better handling chassis than the 'Kwak' – and looked better, too.

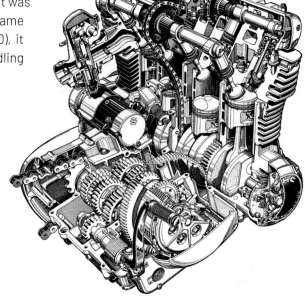

WHO LOVED IT?

The GS750 heralded Suzuki's joining the 'top table' of Japanese four-stroke superbike manufacturers, led directly to the GS1000, and was fast, a fine-handler and affordable. It was succeeded by the four-valve GSX750 and went out of production in 1983.

The GS750's engine was so good some cynics suggested much of its technology and even some of its dimensions were copied from the Kawasaki Z1. In reality it was lighter and more refined. (Suzuki)

It's a black day for other 750 4-strokes.

Pity the competition.

Bad enough they have to contend with Suzuki's super-fast GS-750.

Now they have to face the super-fancy GS-750E. As you can see, it flaunts the blackest paint job this side of midnight. It also sports such fancy plumage as mag-style wheels. Dual-passenger custom seat. Twin disc brakes up front. And high-performance tires.

Power is supplied by a 4-cylinder Dual Overhead Cam engine that boasts 12-second quarters. But, despite the beastly power, you can expect infrequent trips to the gas pumps. And you can expect long trips between pumps thanks to the 4.8 gallon tank.

Six-inch traveling front forks and 5-way adjustable rear shocks soak up the bumps. And to help make our 750 the best handling bike in its class, there's a swingarm that pivots on needle bearings.

Electronic digital indicator tells you what gear you're in. And a tach that redlines at 9000 rpm tells you what gear you should be in.

No need to fret about adjusting the cam chain because it self-adjusts automatically. Nor is there need to worry about leaving the 750E in a parking lot. Because it comes with a new combination ignition and steering lock.

Now you know why this black beauty is making our competitors see red.

SUZUKI
The Fast One.

Ride safely: wear a helmet, eye protection and appropriate riding apparel.

For once, the advertising boasts were spot-on. The press raved about the new Suzuki and its basic architecture and layout paved the way for a whole new generation of four-stroke, four-cylinder Suzukis. (Author's collection)

The press raved, with *Cycle World* declaring it the 'quickest and best-handling 750 on the market' and *Cycle Guide* pitting it against Kawasaki's Z1000 and finding it only half a second slower over the standing quarter mile, but with better handling and with better brakes.

Sales success followed quickly, so much so that Suzuki hastily followed it up with equally impressive 1000 and 550 versions and, by the decade's end, a four-valve 'GSX', which formed the basis of a whole new era of Suzuki four-stroke dominance leading to the legendary GSX-Rs. But without the first GS750 none of it would have been possible – indeed Suzuki might not have survived at all.

WHAT THEY SAID

'The GS is unobtrusively styled, fast, a good handler, comfortable, refined without being futuristic and almost perfect. Some people will say it's a damned good first effort. I'd say it's simply a brilliant motorcycle.'

Bike magazine, March 1977, on the £1,260 Suzuki GS750

With class-leading performance and handling, the biggest criticism levelled at the GS750 was its slightly conservative styling, although this would be improved on later models. (Suzuki)

YAMAHA XS750, 1976

Yamaha was the last of the new Japanese 'Big Four' manufacturers to come up with a big, multi-cylinder four-stroke in the 1970s. As ever, when it did come up with something, it did things differently. (Yamaha)

With the dominance of the new breed of superbike four-stroke fours from the nascent Japanese manufacturers during the 1970s – bikes like Honda's CB750, Kawasaki's Z1 900 and Suzuki's new GS, which would soon be disparaged as UJMs (Universal Japanese Motorcycles) – it's easy to forget that one of the best and most significant Japanese machines of the decade was a shaft-drive triple: Yamaha's XS750.

Although, like Suzuki, Yamaha by the early 1970s was almost entirely associated with two-strokes, the 1976 XS750 wasn't its first big four-stroke. But its earlier XS-1 (later XS650), though reliable, was an 'old school' design and the 1972 TX750 twin an unreliable disaster. Instead, as the mid-1970s approached, Yamaha needed to come back with a big four-stroke 'bang' to avoid being left behind.

The result was the XS750 and Yamaha again did things differently. While its Japanese rivals were all chain-drive, four-stroke fours, the XS was a shaft-drive triple. With a fairly pedestrian 64bhp, it was no rocket, and with shaft drive it wasn't a lightweight sportster, either. But it was smooth, comfortable and reliable, with decent handling; overall, it was more than enough to get Yamaha a place at the top table.

WHAT THEY SAID

'Would I buy it? You better believe I would. Whatever price Yamaha put on their XS750 it's going to be worth it, especially if you're in the market for a luxury cruiser with sporting capabilities.'

Motor Cyclist magazine, October 1977, on the $2,198 Yamaha XS750

Yamaha's all-new XS750 may have also been a four-stroke, 750cc 'multi' with its cylinders arranged transversely across the frame, but it was also a triple, not a four, and had shaft not chain drive. (Yamaha)

With optional cast-alloy wheels, a striking silver/black two-tone paint option and blacked-out engine, the XS750 looked different to all the other Japanese 750/4s, too. (Yamaha)

The XS was classy, too. It had then-novel self-cancelling indicators, soon came with stylish cast wheels, disc brakes front *and* rear and it was sufficiently well received to spawn a series of updates and spin-offs including a custom edition and, in 1980, a larger XS850.

By then, however, having also been joined by the four-cylinder XS1100 in 1978 and, in 1980, the even more impressive XJ650, Yamaha's four-stroke future was assured. But the bike that truly started it rolling was the XS750.

WHO LOVED IT?

Yamaha fans, touring riders and those wanting a Japanese 'multi' that was something different from the four-cylinder sportsters. It remained in production until 1979 when it was replaced by the XS850.

HARLEY-DAVIDSON XLCR, 1977

The last thing anyone expected from US cruiser and touring specialists Harley-Davidson in the late 1970s was a café racer, but that's exactly what the XLCR was intended to be. (Harley-Davidson)

With twenty-first-century Harley-Davidson now finally building modern liquid-cooled adventure bikes alongside its traditional air-cooled, V-twin cruisers, the idea of the American giant making performance sports machines doesn't seem that unusual – but in the 1970s it was a complete anathema. Not that it stopped them.

That bike was the 1977 XLCR 1000. A café racer based on Harley's XL1000 Sportster cruiser, the radical XLCR was the project of H-D design chief Willie G. Davidson who had a fascination with 1960s British café racers and set about building a Harley version for his own personal use. Harley bosses saw it and liked it so much they put it into production.

The bike was unlike any Harley before. Although the XL Sportster engine, frame and front suspension were unchanged, the CR got slightly more 'sports' by way of twin disc front brakes and the swing arm and twin shocks from Harley's XR750 flat-track racer. Everything else was all new. Styling comprised a racy 'bikini' fairing and solo seat, small squared-off tank and front

WHAT THEY SAID

'What you do on the CR is climb aboard this giant old engine, wrap your limbs around whatever falls to hand, foot and knee, and thunder away as close to Jay Springsteen as we mortals will ever come. As a motorcycle, the XLCR has not much merit. As an adventure, the XLCR has no equal.'

Cycle World magazine, May 1977, on the $3,595 Harley-Davidson XLCR-1000

mudguard, all finished off in glossy black paint. The XLCR's riding position was equally extreme, with rear-set pegs and flat one-piece bars.

Trouble was, although striking and sporty, the XLCR's performance was little changed. It may have been - just - Harley's fastest bike, but with just 61bhp it was slower than the new breed of Japanese UJMs and its handling couldn't match Britain's latest twins, such as Norton's Commando. Worst of all, it was more expensive than both and had little appeal to Harley's traditional cruiser customers.

As a result, it was withdrawn from production after just two years due to dismal sales. Today, however, the XLCR's striking looks and rarity make it one of the most desirable 'classic' Harleys of all.

Based on the then 1,000cc sportster V-twin and with all-new, jet-black bodywork, the XLCR looked fantastic. Unfortunately its performance couldn't live up to that promise. (Harley-Davidson)

Sales were so bad that the XLCR was withdrawn from production after barely two years. Today, however, its rarity and beauty make it one of the most collectable of all 1970s Harleys. (Author's collection)

WHO LOVED IT?

Many loved the look but few loved the performance and price. After its 1977 release, the XLCR failed to capture the American public's imagination and it went under-appreciated with press and public alike. Only 1,923 were sold in 1977, 1,201 in 1978 and just 9 in 1979.

3

THE AGE OF THE UJM

By 1977, big four-cylinder UJMs dominated European biking, leading to increasingly sporty and distinctive spin-offs such as Kawasaki's Z1-R. (Kawasaki)

HARLEY-DAVIDSON FXS LOW RIDER, 1977

Today, Harley-Davidsons are synonymous with classic American V-twin cruisers or customs such as the Wide Glide, Fat Boy and Softail – but it all started with the 1977 Low Rider.

Up to the 1970s, Harley was most famous for tourers such as the ElectraGlide, introduced in 1964, and smaller Sportsters first launched in 1957.

By the late 1960s, however, the US customising scene – where bikers 'chopped' their machines, fitting lowered or 'hardtail' rear ends with fat tyres, extended, kicked-out forks with skinny front wheels, stepped seats, 'sissy bar' backrests and 'ape-hanger' handlebars – was in full swing, popularised by movies such as 1969's *Easy Rider*.

Harley's styling director, Willie G. Davidson, was aware of this and set about designing a production bike inspired by these 'choppers'. He married the chassis and engine of the FLH ElectraGlide with the skinny front end of the XLH Sportster and called the result the FX, standing for Factory Experimental. This then gained buckhorn bars

After the failure of the XLCR (and earlier Super Glide) Harley needed a big hit – it got it with the FXS Low Rider. (Harley-Davidson)

WHO LOVED IT?

An instant hit in the US – it was Harley-Davidson's best-selling bike of 1977 – the Low Rider was the first successful factory custom and so popular it redirected the future of Harley towards cruisers and retro-styled bikes.

The Low Rider was Harley's biggest-selling bike of 1977, in turn leading to a series of spin-offs that collectively changed the direction Harley took over the next thirty years. (Harley-Davidson)

and controversial rear bodywork that became known as the 'boat tail'. The resulting bike, the FX Super Glide, was released in 1971. Today it's considered the first 'factory custom'.

It wasn't a success, the rear bodywork in particular being disliked. But Harley persevered and in February 1977 it unveiled the FXS Low Rider, a far better looking and more convincing 'custom' with lowered rear end (hence the name), extended forks and dramatic styling that included cast alloy wheels and even white-lettered tyres.

The new Low Rider was an immediate hit and so loved in the US that it didn't just spawn a succession of new Harley cruisers but changed the direction of the entire company, setting Harley on the path of cruisers, customs (and tourers and Sportsters) it trod almost exclusively for the next thirty years.

The Low Rider was a blend of Harley's ElectraGlide and Sportster but with a look all its own, and is today considered as the first successful 'factory custom'. (Harley-Davidson)

WHAT THEY SAID

'All our critical criteria evaporate when they're levelled against this machine's basic reason for being. If the Low Rider wasn't made out of such solid stuff we can easily imagine it being turned out in the New York garment district. It's apparel, not transportation. You don't really ride a Low Rider; you wear it.'

Cycle World, February 1978, on the $4,180 Harley-Davidson Low Rider

SUZUKI GS1000, 1977

Suzuki's GS750 proved such a success it was no surprise that it was quickly joined by a bigger, even more powerful and successful brother soon afterwards – the GS1000. (Suzuki)

Suzuki truly came of age in the 1970s, first with the four-cylinder GS750 in 1976, the company's first four-stroke after the debacle of the RE-5 rotary, which followed the mostly smaller two-strokes it had made its name with, and then, even more significantly, with the GS1000.

Based on the already brilliant 750, the GS1000 fundamentally changed the perceptions of what UJMs – the disparaging term commonly then used for the new breed of transverse-mounted, four-cylinder Japanese superbikes which were fast but also heavy and handled badly – were capable of.

Although very similar to that of the GS750, the 1000's larger 997cc, two-valve, four-cylinder engine was also lighter and shorter, largely due to its crank having non-circular 'webs' rather than full flywheels and also doing without the 750's kick-starter and shaft.

WHAT THEY SAID

'There aren't many bikes that offer everything in one package. The GS1000 does. Even without its low price tag the Suzuki GS1000 would still be one of the best value-for-money superbikes on our roads today. A true winner.'

Motor Cycle Monthly, July 1978, on the £1,725 Suzuki GS1000

Although based on the GS750 and with a bigger displacement, the GS1000 motor was actually shorter and lighter, helping it become an even better-handling machine. (Suzuki)

The overall result was not just the best-performing bike on the street, it also became the go-to production bike for racers. (Suzuki)

WHO LOVED IT?

Suzuki followed up its sensational GS750 with a new superbike king. The GS1000 was fast, fine handling, affordable and leapfrogged Kawasaki and Honda to be the superbike to have on road or track.

On top of that, although a full-size machine with fairly generic UJM styling, the GS1000 was also lighter than its Japanese rivals, had a comparatively stiff chassis and benefitted from quality air-assisted forks and adjustable rear shocks.

The result was not just a class-leading 90bhp, making the GS easily capable of 130mph, but also, for the first time, the assured handling and cornering ability to match. It was all enough to make the new GS1000 not just the new king on the street but on track as well, winning both the 1978 Daytona 200 and Suzuka 8 Hours and going on to win two AMA Superbike championships (in 1979 and 1980).

Unsurprisingly it was a huge sales success, leading not just to a series of successful spin-offs including the GS1000S and shaft-drive GS1000G, but also 1980's new four-valve GSX1100, which cemented Suzuki's stature as then superbike kings.

KAWASAKI Z1-R, 1978

If your preferred Japanese superbike in the 1970s was Kawasaki's Z1 900 or derivatives such as the enlarged Z1000, then the ultimate, on paper at least, was the 1978 Z1-R.

The first of a new breed of Kawasakis with more modern, angular styling, the Z1-R also had a pioneering handlebar fairing (the first Japanese superbike to do so, a year before Suzuki's GS1000S), slimline 13-litre fuel tank, with the bodywork finished in a striking metallic bluey-silver. In 1978 no Japanese four looked so futuristic.

By the late 1970s, Kawasaki's original king, the Z1 900 (later Z900 and Z1000) had been overtaken by the likes of Suzuki's GS1000. The uprated, restyled Z1-R was its short-lived response. (Kawasaki)

WHAT THEY SAID

'The Z1-R was born to keep the Kawasaki name to the fore at a time when the other Japanese big fours were drawing attention with their own multi-cylinder big guns like the CBX Honda and XS1100 Yamaha.'

Which Bike?, June 1979, on the £2,049 Kawasaki Z1-R

But the Z1-R wasn't 'all show and no go'. Although its 1,015cc two-valve four-cylinder motor was the same as that of the standard Z1000A2, a move to 28mm carbs (from 26mm) plus a four-into-one exhaust helped raise power from 83 to 90bhp, making it the most powerful 'Zed' yet.

Nor was it about just the engine. The chassis was uprated with smart, seven-spoke alloy wheels (the front now 18in instead of the Z1000's 19).

The front and rear brake discs were drilled, race-style, to aid cooling, while it also got the new, self-cancelling indicators. In short the Z1-R went well and looked even better.

Unfortunately, however, the Z1-R may have been great-looking, but it wasn't a success. Outpaced and out-handled by Suzuki's new GS1000, the Kawasaki was also £300 more expensive. Poor sales led to a revised version for 1979 with a larger tank and four-into-two exhaust, but the Z1-R was dropped completely in 1980 when Kawasaki's new 998cc Z1000H debuted. Although more 'restyled stop-gap' than true superbike sensation, the Z1-R was still widely envied and in modern times its striking style, top specification and rarity has made it a desirable 1970s classic.

The Z1-R was more powerful, slimmer, better handling, better looking and a true 1970s dream machine, but underneath all of that was a fairly old-tech motorcycle. (Kawasaki)

WHO LOVED IT?

Although futuristic and fast enough to be a true poster bike of the late 1970s, being £300 more expensive than the faster and better-handling GS1000 restricted sales and the Z1-R was taken off sale after just two years.

With *Star Wars*-style silver paint (and accompanying silver-clad model), drilled brake discs and sexy nose fairing, the Z1-R was still one of the most lusted-after bikes of 1978. (Kawasaki)

HONDA CBX1000, 1978

By 1978, Honda fans had been waiting a long time for a true superbike successor to the old SOHC CB750. So when the DOHC, six-cylinder 1000cc CBX arrived, it caused a sensation. (Honda)

No motorcycle of the 1970s was as ambitious, extravagant and downright fantastic as Honda's glorious six-cylinder CBX. Conceived in early 1976, the CBX was launched in 1978 to mark ten years since Honda's original superbike, the CB750 – but it was also so much more.

With Suzuki and Yamaha also starting to explore 750cc four-strokes, the aging CB750 outpaced, and with a '60s four-stroke racing legacy of five- and even six-cylinder machines, Honda decided to re-establish its superbike supremacy with the ultimate incarnation of the CB lineage.

After considering a four-cylinder 1000 and 1200, an all-new, 1,048cc six designed by Shoichiro Irimajiri, the man behind those '60s racers, was agreed. The four-cylinder, meanwhile, was continued by another team and would become the CB900F.

In truth, the CBX wasn't the first production six – that plaudit went to Benelli's 750 Sei in 1973 – but at 1,048cc, with 105bhp and a top speed of 130mph, it was the biggest, most powerful and fastest. And with double overhead cams, four valves per cylinder and six exquisite 28mm carburettors, it was

also the most sophisticated. A tubular spine frame was created from which the massive motor was hung to show the engine at its best. It had 35mm forks, disc brakes all round and Honda's latest pressed-aluminium Comstar wheels.

Launched at the Suzuka race circuit in November 1977, the first production machines arrived at dealers in March 1978 and examples were used by travelling marshals at that year's TT – when Mike Hailwood returned to grab his fairy-tale win.

But although a true 'poster bike', the CBX was also too expensive and excessive to be a commercial success – even when later adapted into a sports tourer with monoshock suspension and touring fairing. (Honda)

Today it's the early, first-generation CBX1000s, as inspired by Honda's six-cylinder racers of the 1960s, that are the most desirable and collectable. (Honda)

WHAT THEY SAID

'The CBX is a welcome, if exclusive, addition to motorcycling. Honda say it's their ultimate and it's difficult to imagine anything faster ... It's a much-needed boost for Honda and bikes in general for it shows that exciting, glamourous motorcycles can be made in Japan.'

Bike magazine, December 1978, on the £2,750 Honda CBX1000

But despite all the positive publicity, the CBX proved a slow seller. Although it caused a sensation wherever it was seen, the CBX cost an enormous £2,750, and its performance and complexity meant few insurance companies were willing to provide cover.

Worse, in 1979 Honda themselves launched the CB900F, with 95bhp, more agile handling and a far cheaper price tag. By year's end, unsold CBXs were being discounted by dealers by up to £1,000.

Reinvented as a faired, panniered tourer for 1981, the CBX limped on before finally being dropped in 1982. Commercially, Honda's magnificent six had been a failure. But as a statement, flagship machine and a technical tour de force, the 1970s saw nothing better.

WHO LOVED IT?

Although the CBX caused a sensation, commercially, with Honda's own CB900F faster, more agile and cheaper, it was a disaster, even when reinvented as a faired, Pro-Linked tourer. A total of 38,079 were built in Japan with 3,150 more built in the US at Honda's Ohio factory.

YAMAHA XS1100, 1978

By 1978, with Suzuki's GS1000 joining Kawasaki's Z1000 and Honda's CBX1000, it seemed 1970s superbikes had reached their limit. Then Yamaha trumped them all with its all-new XS1100 which, briefly, was the biggest, fastest production motorcycle in the world.

Realising its first four-stroke 'multi', the 1977 XS750, needed a bigger brother, the new four-cylinder was a direct development of the shaft-drive, DOHC triple but surprised by being, at 1,101.6cc, larger than the 1000 expected. It also benefitted from the new Mikuni Constant Velocity (CV) carbs and employed a new combustion chamber design.

The result produced not only an impressive 95bhp but delivered, in the hands of *Cycle* magazine in January 1978, a standing quarter-mile time of just 11.82 seconds. A month later, US rival *Cycle World* posted 11.78 seconds. Motorcycling had a new quarter-mile king.

WHAT THEY SAID

'I really do wonder where this crazy helter-skelter is taking us as manufacturers seem unable to look beyond the statistics of top speed and quarter mile times. Don't they know that some of these behemoths are not terribly pleasant to ride if you're not Clark Kent?'

Bike magazine, December 1978, on the £2,110 Yamaha XS1100

Even undressed, Yamaha's new shaft-drive superbike was clearly heavy and cumbersome, but it was also undeniably fast, breaking numerous straight-line acceleration records. (Yamaha)

WHO LOVED IT?

In 1978 if you wanted the biggest, fastest Japanese four-cylinder superbike, then the XS1100 was (briefly) it. Unfortunately, it was also so heavy that if you wanted to carve through corners you were better off looking elsewhere. Production numbers aren't known.

Unfortunately, that was as good as it got. The XS1100 was also so heavy its handling suffered, with high-speed wobbles in turns commonly reported. In 1979 a special faired UK version was painted in Martini colours to tie-in with Mike Hailwood's TT comeback, but that year the XS1100's biggest/most powerful crown was also taken by Kawasaki's new Z1300 six.

The XS limped on with a custom version launched in the US and, in 1981, a handlebar-faired 'S' sports version, but its time was up. A development of the engine was, however, used in Yamaha's 1983 FJ1100/1200, which lived on as a superlative sports tourer well into the mid-1990s.

Although heavy, with 95bhp on tap (and a madman at the controls), the XS1100 could even be persuaded to do stunts! (Yamaha)

HONDA CX500, 1978

In 1978 Honda launched one of the most technologically advanced and successful motorcycles of the decade. No, not the glamourous, fantastic CBX-6 but the far more humdrum, often reviled, yet massively popular CX500.

Conceived to replace the aging CB500/4, CB550/4 and CB500T, the CX500, also called the 500 Wing in the US, was designed by Shoichiro Irimajiri, the man responsible for both the GL1000 and CBX. Like those bikes, it was impressively innovative – except this time it wasn't in the pursuit of power. The result, Honda's first V-twin with liquid-cooling, shaft drive and Comstar wheels (which allowed the use of tubeless tyres), was unlike any motorcycle seen before.

It also boasted a series of clever design features. To avoid the transverse V-twin's carbs hitting the rider's knees, its heads were twisted 22 degrees, with the four valves operated by push-rods to allow this.

WHO LOVED IT?

In production in various forms up to 1984, the versatile, affordable CX500 proved massively popular. Some 186,000 standard CX500s were sold, along with 30,000 Silver Wing variants, 21,000 CX650s and 7,000 of the later Turbo version. In total, over 300,000 were sold, making it one of the most popular bikes of all time.

Unfortunately, the CX also looked unlike any previous motorcycle, with the end result initially baffling some stateside testers and drawing criticism for being underwhelming and ugly. 'Plastic maggot' was one catcall that stuck.

In the UK the CX went down a storm. *Motor Cycle Weekly* called it a pacesetter in rider comfort, handling, performance and quietness. *Two Wheels* magazine in Australia made the CX their bike of the year, and sales to those wanting a rugged, reliable all-rounder went through the roof. Custom and Silver Wing touring versions followed, along with a 650 and even a Turbo in the 1980s.

The CX was spun-off into 650 and even turbo and cruiser variants and remained on sale until 1984, becoming one of Honda's best-selling models of all time. (Author's collection)

With a modest but tractable power delivery, practical shaft drive and quirky looks (it later became nicknamed the 'Plastic Maggot') the CX was never a poster bike – but it did become hugely popular. (Honda)

WHAT THEY SAID

'The CX500 has proved to me to be without doubt the best all-rounder for general use. The advantages are as follows: shaft-drive reliability; high seating position; superb lights front and rear and the most tractable engine I have yet come across.'

Which Bike?, November 1979, on the £1,330 Honda CX500

SUZUKI PE175, 1978

If Suzuki's main success of the late 1970s was its new GS four-strokes, its most significant machines through much of the rest of the decade were two-strokes, particularly in the off-road world with its RM motocrossers, TS trail machines and, arguably most desirably of all, the enduro 'PE' bikes, which fitted between the two.

After a series of competent two-stroke trail bikes in the late 1960s, Suzuki hit the big time when it targeted world motocross, wooed reigning 250cc champion Joel Robert and won the 1970 250cc world crown. Robert retained it for the next two years. For 1971, meanwhile, Suzuki also hired Belgian compatriot Roger De Coster for the blue riband 500cc class aboard their new, lightweight TM400 (which De Coster helped develop) and promptly won that title, too. De Coster also retained that for the next two years.

Suzuki had risen to the very top of world motocross during the early 1970s, while its TS trail bikes had also proved popular. Its 1978 PE175 blended the best of both worlds. (Suzuki)

WHO LOVED IT?

The ultimate production 'enduro', Suzuki's PE blended grand-prix-winning motocross technology and performance with Suzuki's already class-leading TS trail bike manners. The PEs were never huge sellers, but they were the most lusted-after dirt bikes for road riders in the late 1970s.

As a result, through most of the 1970s, Suzuki's TM and RM motocrossers, along with their road-going relatives, the TS trail bikes, were the dirt bikes to be seen on.

Suzuki's masterstroke, however, was the PE – 'Pure Enduro' – series launched in 1977. Available in 175, 250 and 400cc forms, they were basically RM motocrossers (the 175 being an enlarged 125) with minimal lighting and instruments to make them road legal. Suzuki altered the gearing and porting, and gave them a heavier flywheel to make them more flexible, and yet the PE maintained virtually all the brazen yellow race style and ability of their RM cousins. This was proven when the British team entered three PE250s in the 1976 International Six Days Trail and promptly won three gold medals.

In the late 1970s, if you wanted a good two-stroke trail bike, you bought a Suzuki TS. But if you wanted the dirt equivalent of Barry Sheene's RG GP bike, you wanted a PE, and the 175 was the most accessible of them all.

With near MX levels of power, a lightweight chassis yet manners most could manage, the PE175 was a true pin-up machine. (Author's collection)

WHAT THEY SAID

'The PE is easier to ride faster than you might expect of ultra-competitive enduro mounts, it handles deftly and precisely and appears to be tough as nails.'

Which Bike?, November 1978, on the £825 Suzuki PE175

Although most popular in mid-range 175cc form, the PE 'Pure Enduro' was also available in fiercer 250 and even 400cc forms. (Author's collection)

HONDA CB250N/400N, 1978

Looking back, it is hard to imagine the humble Honda Super Dream could be a 'loved bike of the 1970s', but the classy, learner 250 was one of the best-selling bikes of the late 1970s. (Honda)

The CB250N was launched at the same time as its slightly bigger brother, the CB400N. Both had effective (if uninspiring) four-stroke parallel-twin motors, 'Eurostyle' looks and a reputation for quality and durability. (Honda)

Few motorcycles of the 1970s were as popular – but at the same time as derided – as the CB250N Super Dream launched in 1978.

Commonly mocked as the 'Wet Dream', Honda's successor to the short-lived Dream 250 was a SOHC four-stroke twin aimed at the then hugely popular learner 250 market. The new Super got a new six-speed transmission but, more significantly, swoopy new integrated 'Eurostyling'. This was then carried though its range including the 250's bigger brother, the CB400N, and, most mouth-wateringly, Honda's new twin-cam CB750F and CB900F fours.

In truth, the Honda 250 wasn't as 'Super' as all that suggests. Its handling suffered from fairly hefty weight, its single-cam twin was a little soft and capable of only 27bhp and barely 90mph (Suzuki's later twin-cam GSX250 of 1980 produced 29bhp), and all were outpaced by sportier, 100mph, two-stroke 250s such as Suzuki's 1978 GT250X7 and Yamaha's 1980 RD250LC.

For learner buyers (or commuters), few bikes gave as convincing a 'big bike' experience for so little money as Honda's CB250N/400N Super Dream duo. (Author's collection)

In reality, though, none of that mattered. The CB250N looked great; was a substantial, credible and versatile 'first big bike'; and, best of all, being a Honda, it had an impeccable reputation for reliability and was available through the UK's most extensive dealer network.

WHAT THEY SAID

'If nothing else the Honda was the most impressive for its striking appearance and sweeping style. It looks what it is, a big bike.'

Which Bike?, June 1979, on the £849 Honda CB250N

Sales took off, making the Super Dream not just the most popular learner 250 of the late 1970s but, at the start of the 1980s, Britain's most popular bike. That was extended by the introduction of a higher spec Deluxe variant from 1981 until the 250 class was effectively killed off by a new 125cc learner law introduced in 1983. During those late 1970s learner 250 years, however, the CB250N Super Dream was king.

WHO LOVED IT?

The versatile, good-looking, solid, classy and, crucially, learner-legal CB250N was one of Honda's best-selling bikes of the late 1970s, selling 70,000 in the UK alone up to 1983 and 17,000 just in 1980.

With just 27bhp on tap (from the 250 version) 'European Race Bikes' may have been stretching the definition too far. Instead, for many the Super Dream became known as the 'Wet Dream'. (Author's collection)

SUZUKI GT250X7, 1978

Due to the 250cc UK learner law, quarter-litre machines – particularly sporty, fast and Japanese ones – were hugely popular in the 1970s. And the sportiest and fastest of all, at least from 1978 until 1980, was Suzuki's GT250X7.

Throughout most of the decade, although Suzuki had its decent GT250 stroker twin and Kawasaki its even more potent KH250 triple, the undoubted king of sports learner bikes was Yamaha's long-reigning RD250. Updated in 1976

After years of 250 stroker dominance by Yamaha's RD250 twin, Suzuki finally snatched the learner sports crown with its ultralight GT250X7. (Suzuki)

into its most famous 'coffin-tanked' form, then gaining the snazzy alloy wheels to go with its class leading 30bhp, the RD had the beating of the 28bhp KH and larger Suzuki.

But that all changed with the GT's successor. Instead of chasing power, the X7 got its performance boost by being a smaller and, crucially, lighter machine. Although power was unchanged at 28bhp, the all-new X7 motor had better midrange and was much more compact and a full 7.2kg lighter than its predecessor.

The new 'Ton-up' Suzuki GT250X7
A 250 has never looked so good

The latest Suzuki 250 doesn't exactly hang about. Its top speed is around 100mph.

But speed is only half the story.

Our new 250 has got a lot more going for it. Like superb handling. (Back at the factory, Suzuki engineers have got weight distribution down to a fine art).

What else?

An all-new "Power Reed" engine. Pointless ignition.

Spot-on braking with beefy discs up front. 6-speed gearbox. Lightweight frame. Alloy wheels. Totally new styling.

See the quickest-ever 250 at your Suzuki Dealer. And get away from the pack

Yes, you can believe your eyes.

The getaway bike has never looked so good. Or performed so well.

Superbly balanced frame.
Lightweight yet very strong

Alloy wheels

Pointless ignition
for faultless performance

6-speed gearbox

All-new "Power Reed" 2-stroke twin

TEXACO
HERON
TEAM SUZUKI

HERON SUZUKI

the getaway bike

Although no more powerful than the rival Yamaha, the new X7 was lighter, sleeker, better handling and sharper looking. Some press reports, meanwhile, claimed it was capable of 100mph. (Suzuki)

Although fast, fine-handling and popular on both street and track, the X7 was also fairly 'old tech' with twin-shock suspension and chrome styling. (Suzuki)

The X7's twin-shock chassis, though conventional, was more compact and much lighter, too, while all-new styling, although continuing with the 1970s convention of twin shocks and lashings of chrome, was more angular and purposeful.

The result was sharp, light, aggressive and powerful enough to nudge 100mph, making it the fastest 250 of the day, while Suzuki cemented its new status by offering an equally purposeful 200 version – the X5. It might not have lasted long, but in 1978–80, if you wanted the fastest, sharpest learner bikes around, you wanted a Suzuki.

WHO LOVED IT?

Learner sports stroker loons and proddie racers loved the X7, even if its reign was short-lived – Yamaha's all-new, liquid-cooled RD250LC stealing its crown in 1980. The X7 was superseded by the even racier RG250 in 1983, but by then the 250 learner law had changed and sales as a result were limited.

The X7 ruled the late 1970s learner sports-bike roost until the arrival of the Yamaha RD250LC in 1980. A smaller version, the GT200X5, was also popular. (Suzuki)

LAVERDA MONTJUIC 500, 1979

Following Laverda's success with its 1,000cc three-cylinder Jota, the Italian marque followed it up with an equally fearsome middleweight, the 500cc twin-cylinder Montjuic. (Laverda)

If the legendary Laverda Jota 1,000cc triple was the 1970s most fearsome Italian superbike, then its later little brother, the Montjuic 500cc twin, was its middleweight mimic. No mid-range machine of the decade was so riotous, fierce – and *loud*!

The Montjuic was created in similar circumstances to the big Jota. In September 1975, the Italian marque unveiled the prototype of its new middleweight twin and the motorcycling press dreamed of a baby Jota. It was not to be – not yet, anyway.

When the Alpina 500 hit the road in 1977, its performance was disappointing, prompting Laverda to create a one-make race series in Italy, the 'Coppa Laverda', using stripped-down and tuned versions, dubbed the Formula 500, to promote its sporting abilities.

Meanwhile in the UK, poor Alpina sales prompted UK importers Slater Brothers, who had also been behind the creation of the Jota, to lobby the factory to combine elements of the Formula 500 with the Alpina. Then, when the resultant bikes arrived in the UK, Slater Brothers added a UK-made race seat and fairing. The result was the raciest road-going Italian middleweight of the day with the loud exhaust to match.

The Montjuic's 500cc parallel-twin engine was tuned and fitted with a race exhaust that proved so loud the little Laverda was legislated off the road after just two years. (Author's collection)

With its race single seat, handlebar fairing and top-spec brakes, wheels and suspension, no middleweight of the late 1970s was as sporty as the Laverda Montjuic 500. (Laverda)

WHAT THEY SAID

'The Montjuic is bound for a place in the motorcycling history books. Its tuned motor produces 55bhp, Laverdas have always been favoured for their good handling but the Montjuic raises the standard to new heights, but it's LOUD.'

Which Bike?, October 1979, on the £2,095 Laverda Montjuic 500

WHO LOVED IT?

A 'junior Jota', a pure-bred race bike for the road with the handling (and exhaust note) to match, the Montjuic was also outpaced by most Japanese middleweight fours and was expensive and anti-social. Laverda made fewer than 3,000 examples of its 500 twin with an estimated 250–300 converted to Montjuics.

Although a success despite its hefty price tag, in reality the Montjuic was also something of an anomaly and was never destined to live long. Although brisk, its twin-cylinder performance couldn't match that of most of the middleweight Japanese fours at a fraction of the price. Although a fine handler, it was so extreme it had none of the civility to make sense as a road bike and its 105db fell foul of the law makers such that the junior Laverda was legislated off the road within two years. But, boy, what a blast it was while it was there.

Suzuki's limited-edition S version of its all-conquering GS1000 was intended to give its 1,000cc
four the sporting style and specification to match its race success – it worked. (Suzuki)

The late 1970s were glorious years for Suzuki's new four-stroke four-cylinder motorcycles. But after the mould-breaking GS750 of 1976, followed up by the 1977 GS1000 (which became the new litre-class benchmark), not to mention middleweight all-rounders such as the GS550, the best was saved for decade's end with the mouth-watering and exclusive GS1000S.

Although those earlier bikes were exceptional, they still left a need unfulfilled. Until the 1000S, although Suzuki's fours were fast, fine-handling and fabulous value, they lacked the style and sheer visual drama of, say, a Kawasaki. The GS 'thou' may have had the beating of the Z1000, as proven by American Wes Cooley's race towards the 1979 AMA Superbike title aboard a Yoshimura-tuned version, but bikes like Kawasaki's Z1-R *looked* faster. Simply mention 'performance Japanese machine' to any '70s bike nut and odds are the name 'Kawasaki' would bounce back.

The GS1000S was created to change all that. Although fundamentally a standard GS1000, the S gave the GS a racy pizazz the standard bike didn't have. A limited-edition machine intended to homologate performance features for Cooley's 1980 campaign, it became, in so doing, the first production Suzuki to feature a fairing (a stylish, handlebar design which also gained a clock), a larger 18in rear wheel (compared to the previous 17-incher), uprated suspension and Suzuki racing livery in either white/blue or white/red.

WHO LOVED IT?

The S was the ultimate version of the already class-leading GS1000. Fast, fine handling and mouth-watering to look at, it was the ultimate Suzuki superbike of the late 1970s. Around 7,000 were built.

In the US, the GS1000 had already won the AMA Superbike championship in 1979 in the hands of Wes Cooley.
He repeated the feat on the S in 1980, leading to the new bike becoming dubbed the 'Wes Cooley Replica'. (Suzuki)

WHAT THEY SAID

'The Suzuki reflects the factory racing efforts and does so with their racing colours of blue and white the livery used on the RG500 two-stroke fours as sold.'

Which Bike?, June 1979, on the £2,045 Suzuki GS1000S

Unveiled at the end of 1979, the S, with the suffix signifying Sport, was an instant sensation. It went on to power Cooley to a second title in 1980 (so inspiring the 'Wes Cooley replica' nickname it acquired) and was immediately the most desirable – Honda CBX arguably aside – of all UJMs. That mantle may not have lasted long – Suzuki's own first four-valve GSX1100 debuted later in 1980 – but in the final year of the 1970s, the GS1000S was one of the most loved motorcycles. Among collectors, it remains so today.

With its distinctive handlebar fairing and GP race bike replica white/blue or white/red livery, the GS1000S was one of the most distinctive – and now collectable – Japanese superbikes of all. (Suzuki)

HONDA CB900FZ, 1979

By the late 1970s, Honda's original SOHC CB750, as launched in 1969, had been thoroughly eclipsed by its Japanese rivals, first Kawasaki's Z1 900, then Suzuki's GS750 and GS1000, not to mention Yamaha's XS750.

Honda's initial response was drawn out and unconvincing. The restyled 1975 CB750 Super Sport was little more than a stopgap and the 1978 CBX1000 six was too extreme and expensive. Alongside the CBX, however, Honda had been developing

an all-new four-cylinder, which revolutionised the class both in terms of technology and style and ushered in a new superbike era.

Launched in 1979, the DOHC CB900FZ was not only the world's first 16-valve, four-cylinder production bike but its chassis also raised the handling bar, being 9kg lighter and more nimble and secure than Suzuki's reigning GS1000.

The new DOHC, 16-valve, four-cylinder engine was a worthy successor to the old SOHC CB750 and borrowed much of its style and technology from the 'six', which had been developed at the same time. (Honda)

The CB900FZ survived into the 1980s, with later versions gaining uprated brakes and styling updates, including 'reversed' Comstar wheels and blacked-out engines. Variants including the F2 half-faired sports-tourer. (Honda)

WHAT THEY SAID

'The 900 is a far better "bikers bike" than the CBX by virtue of the fact that, although it has a far less impressive specification (which in itself may be looked upon as an advantage), it still performs just as well, handles better and costs a large chunk less.'

Motorcyclist Illustrated, December 1978, on the £1,995 CB900FZ

It looked different, too. Famously targeted more at Europe than the US, the CB900FZ was given swoopy new styling Honda dubbed 'Eurostyle' similar to what had debuted on the previous year's CB250/400N duo, where the tank 'flowed' into the side panels then into the seat unit. Honda's Comstar pressed-aluminium wheels were again used and quality was typically Honda good.

However, although – briefly – the fastest, best-handling superbike around, the CB900FZ, while revered, never quite achieved the recognition or classic status it deserved. Being a Honda, the big four was also refined, versatile and civilised, so much so it actually detracted from its sporting image. Its 95bhp was also quickly overtaken by rivals, with Suzuki's 100bhp GSX1100 arriving the following year.

A slightly baffling marketing decision, meanwhile, saw the CB900FZ debut in Europe in 1979 but not in the US until two years later. Instead, the Americans got the smaller CB750FZ, as famously raced in AMA Superbikes by 'Fast' Freddie Spencer, Honda's reasoning being that the CB900FZ would hit CBX1000 sales in the six-cylinder bike's biggest potential market. It was the Americans' – and Honda's – loss. European riders, however, loved it.

WHO LOVED IT?

Good looking, fast and with a proven badge, the CB900FZ put Honda back on top of the 1970s superbike pile – but only briefly. Suzuki's new GSX1100 would swiftly steal it back in 1980. Until then, however, the CB9 was a big hit, but in Europe only. It didn't go on sale in the US until 1981.

DUCATI MHR 900, 1979

Ducati's MHR (Mike Hailwood Replica) 900 was first produced in 1979 in commemoration of Mike the Bike's legendary 1978 Isle of Man return and victory in the F1 TT. (Ducati)

No motorcycle racing feat of the 1970s was more astonishing and celebrated than Mike 'The Bike' Hailwood's stunning comeback victory at the 1978 TT. And no motorcycle of the decade was more magical and alluring than the replica Ducati built in its honour – the 1979 MHR 900.

Except it wasn't, quite, what it could have been ...

Hailwood's victory, eleven years after his retirement at the ripe old age of 38, aboard a privately entered twin-cylinder Ducati against the full might of a works four-cylinder Honda ridden by 1974 World 500 Champion Phil Read, is the stuff of motorcycle legend.

Unsurprisingly, the Italian factory decided to capitalise on his victory. The MHR 900 certainly looked the part. A 900 bevel-drive V-twin with a full race fairing in faithful Hailwood red, green and white with a special, copycat tank seat unit and uprated rear suspension, clocks and switches. No Italian bike of 1979 was racier – or more lust worthy. An initial 500 were built, selling out instantly.

WHO LOVED IT?

Between 1979 and 1986, more than 7,000 MHRs were built, making it the most numerous of all the bevel-drive twin models – including the 900SS, 750GT and Sport, the 860GT range and the Darmahs.

In truth, the production MHR was little more than a facsimile of Hailwood's racing machine, which was a hand-built, sand-cast case racer produced by NCR, Ducati's unofficial racing arm in Bologna. (Ducati)

In reality, of course, the MHR was little more than Ducati's then 900SS in different bodywork. It bore little resemblance to Hailwood's racer, a hand-built special built by Ducati's racing arm, NCR, but for most that didn't matter.

Buoyed by the bike's success, Ducati turned their 'limited edition' into a full production machine. The 1980 version featured a modified fairing, the 1981 different exhausts and the 1982 new side panels, by which time it had become Ducati's best-selling model. Production finally ended in 1986 and, in truth, none were the performance specials their name and style suggested. But in 1979, as an iconic Italian sporting machine with incomparable racing pedigree, nothing came close to the MHR.

HAILWOOD'S FAIRY TALE

In the 1960s, Mike Hailwood was the world's most successful and highest-paid motorcycle racer, winning nine world championships, seventy-six Grand Prix and living a playboy lifestyle. In 1967, however, in objection to new regulations which banned its multi-cylinder engines, leading team Honda pulled out of motorcycle GP racing and paid star rider Hailwood £50,000 not to ride for any other GP team.

Instead, he turned to one-off rides, including riding for BSA/Triumph at the 1970 Daytona 200, and car racing, achieving two F1 podiums, before retiring to New Zealand in 1974.

In 1978, however, after sampling and being impressed by a Ducati V-twin at a race in Australia the previous year, he accepted an offer from

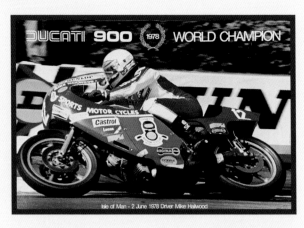

On 2 June 1978, Mike Hailwood, the nine-times champion, who retired from world championship racing in 1968, returned to the TT after a decade away onboard an unfancied Ducati and won against all the odds and against the mighty Honda works team headed by Phil Read. (Ducati)

UK dealer Sports Motorcycles to ride a Ducati in the newly introduced F1 race at the TT. Although a production-based formula, Hailwood's bike was actually a specialist racer built by NCR with a lightweight frame and sand-cast cases. But it was still hugely down on power compared to chief rival Phil Read's Honda. Hailwood himself hadn't raced on the Isle of Man for eleven years, so when he won in June 1978, posting a new lap record in the process, he caused a national sensation.

Hailwood returned the following year, this time narrowly coming second in the F1 race on a revised Ducati the MHR became modelled on and winning the Senior race on a Suzuki RG500 before retiring for good. Tragically he was killed in a car accident in March 1981 while taking his children to get fish and chips.

WHAT THEY SAID

'Excellent though the MHR undoubtedly was, it wasn't a true 900SS somehow. Less scantily clothed and marginally slower at the top end, the Rep was more of a cousin than a brother to the great Ducati progenitor, the 750SS.'

Superbike magazine, November 1979, on the £2,999 Ducati MHR 900

Later MHRs evolved and improved, first with added side panels, then with an increase to 1,000cc and more. But, although glorious and popular, they were all really only rebodied 900SSs. (Ducati)

KAWASAKI Z1300, 1979

If the 1970s are to be remembered for any trends in motorcycling apart from the UJM, surely it is for being a decade of excess. No bikes exemplified 'motorcycling mosts' better than a 'six' and this decade had three of them – the Benelli Sei, Honda CBX and last, but by no means least, Kawasaki's stupendous Z1300.

Many assume Kawasaki's entry into the six-cylindered world to be a direct reaction to the CBX: it wasn't. Instead, in development since 1974, it was conceived as a bigger, non-two-stroke, 'show bike' successor to its own Mach III and Mach IV triples, for whom the death knell rang with the 1973 oil crisis.

A capacity of at least 1,200cc was settled on in response to Honda's GL1000 Gold Wing, an inline-six was decreed to distinguish it from the increasingly commonplace transverse-fours and shaft drive, commissioned from Isuzu, was necessary as no chain was then capable of handling its projected 120bhp. Meanwhile, 1,300cc was settled on in response to Harley's new 1977 1,340cc 'Shovelhead' V-twin.

After being unveiled at the 1978 Cologne Show, the Z1300 did cause a sensation. Unfortunately, part of that was also for being enormous (even its fuel tank was a monster 27 litres), expensive and, at a massive 297kg, heavier than any other machine. As a result, although sensational, sales were slow, unsurprisingly slow in Europe perhaps, but disappointingly so in the US, where it was expected to rival the Honda Wing. The big Kawasaki survived into the 1980s, gaining fuel injection and a further 10bhp in 1983, and the US gaining a 'full dress' tourer version, the Voyager, the same year. But despite also being made in the US, in a special Kawasaki plant in Lincoln, Nebraska, mirroring Honda's Gold Wing practice, it was never the success hoped for, finally going out of production in 1989. In the 1970s, however, no bike had made a bigger impression.

WHAT THEY SAID

'The Z1300 is altogether an extremely thrilling motorcycle to ride. And it is, despite its appearance, a motorcycle in every sense of the word. The only difference between this and others is that there's more of it.'

Which Bike?, October 1979, on the £3,188 Kawasaki Z1300

At the time people assumed the Z13 was a response to Honda's similar six-cylinder CBX1000 – it wasn't. But it was also the end of the line for the enormous capacity, multi-cylinder, power-hungry Japanese monsters that had come to define the late 1970s. (Kawasaki)

Z1300
Kawasaki

Straight-line performance, thrills and acceleration on the Kawasaki Z1300 were, perhaps unsurprisingly, without equal. Sadly actually levering the big six around corners safely was without compare, too. (Kawasaki)

WHO LOVED IT?

Although a sensation and in production in various forms for ten years, the big, expensive Z1300 wasn't a sales success. By 1989 only 20,000 standard versions had been sold, with reports of dealers having them in stock right up to 1993!